JOHN
GIERACH

THE
VIEW
FROM
RAT
LAKE

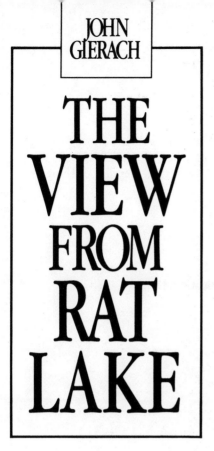

JOHN GIERACH

THE VIEW FROM RAT LAKE

PRUETT *P* PUBLISHING COMPANY
Boulder, Colorado

First Edition
1 2 3 4 5 6 7 8 9

Library of Congress Cataloging-in-Publication Data

Gierach, John, 1946–
   The view from Rat Lake.

   1. Fly fishing. 2. Trout fishing. I. Title.
SH456.G58 1988   799.1′755   88-5926
ISBN 0-87108-743-X Regular edition
ISBN 0-87108-749-9 Limited edition

Briefer versions of "On the Ice," "Transitions," "Enough Fish," and "All This Will be Underwater," were first published in *Field & Stream*, *Rod & Reel*, and *Flyfishing* magazines, respectively. "The Fishing Car" was published in its entirety in *Gray's Sporting Journal*.

CONTENTS

"I can report that pleasure wears well."
Andy Rooney

"In my limited way of seeing things, I feel this will go on forever."
Russell Chatham

"If the trout are lost, smash the state."
Thomas McGuane

I n the world of fishing there are magic phrases that are guaranteed to summon the demon. Among them are: "remote trout lake," "fish up to 13 pounds," "the place the guides fish on their days off," and "my travel agent."

There's power in words like that.

Place names also help. The purely descriptive ones, like Ship Rock Lake and Lone Pine, are okay, but add poetry or even irony and the effect is heightened. Take Rat Lake for example. A good fisherman can call you up on the phone, rattle off an incantation like that, and make you wrench your elbow going for your checkbook too quickly.

I didn't hurt my elbow, but I did manage to pull a muscle in my back a few days before I was supposed to leave for Rat Lake. And it was one of those scheduled trips, too. I was to meet a friend at his office (yes, I do have some friends with offices), we would drive to the airport, meet a third guy, fly to Bozeman, Montana, to meet a fourth guy, and so on. It was not one that could have been casually put off for a week while your back healed up. You go or you cancel, period.

Now I'm not generally a wuss about these things, but the back was actually quite sore, and I had my doubts about being able to get into a pair of waders and a belly boat without help. I called my kindly old white-haired doc and said, "What the hell should I do?" expecting him to prescribe a vial of pastel-colored miracle pills that would fix it overnight.

"Well," Doc said, "go fishing, and if you catch one that hurts you to lift, break him off. Now, if you'll excuse me, I have *sick people* to take care of."

So, I went fishing. Doctor's orders.

We stayed at a guest ranch, in a sweet little log cabin with a stone fireplace and a big stack of dry wood; and it was a good thing, too, because the famous Big Sky was low and dark and drizzling a cold, steady rain that had an ominously permanent feel to it. When you're far from home at some expense, it's not feasible to wait this kind of thing out in a bar, because you either don't have enough time or are in too much of a hurry. The former just happens to you, while the latter you do to yourself, but they amount to the same thing: you bundle up and fish. That's what you came for. At least there's a warm, dry place to come dragging back to.

From what I'd been told about it, Rat Lake fell into the category that's often described by fishermen as "A son of a bitch." It's not all that difficult to get to if you don't mind slogging uphill on a wet, slimy clay trail with a fully loaded float tube strapped to your back, and it's small enough and shallow enough to fish easily with a fly rod. The problem with Rat Lake, and the other sons of bitches like it, is that you can't catch the fish. Or, more properly, you can only catch a very few of them, and those only by putting in first hours and then days of trying this and that, here and there, always waiting for the caddis hatch, spinner fall, or whatever else it takes for the huge trout of local legend to show themselves.

Lakes like this are considered worth the trouble, especially by those few—usually locals—who have seen and perhaps even caught some of the fish. As it turns out, some guides *do* fish Rat Lake on their days off.

It's the kind of fishing you have to be in the mood for, and I *was* in the mood. It was spring, and I'd been a good boy for most of the winter, working hard on several things, including this book. I figured I owed myself some serious big trout fishing from

2

cushy accommodations because, well, because that's what writers do, isn't it? They finish The Book and then go off to Paris to drink and carouse—or to Montana to fish and drink—to relax, let the well fill up, and prove to themselves once again that they don't really give a damn about much of anything.

At least that's what my study of literature seems to indicate.

Of course, this was in country where grizzly bears are known to live, and we'd spent some time in a bar the evening before trying to scare the one member of the party who had never been to Montana before and had some misgivings in this area. We told him the way to tell a black bear from a grizzly is that the black will follow you up a tree while the griz will just shake you out.

He sipped his "jumper cable" (a local drink that warms you up after a cold day of fishing, but also causes nightmares) and said he was more scared of rattlesnakes than bears. I said, "Sure, but if a rattler gets you, at least they'll find more of you than your shoes."

You probably know that the .44 magnum is the handgun of choice among those who worry about grizzly bears, but did you know that the .357 mag.—no slouch in the deadly weapon department—is known in some circles as a "bear tickler?" "Yes sir, your best chance with the three-five-seven is to shoot the bear with it and then slip away while he's busy laughing."

This is all pretty cruel, I suppose, but it's one of those manly things we men do to each other for no other reason than that it was once done to us. I won't glorify it by calling it a rite of passage.

The following morning we climbed to Rat Lake. We found it to be just above the altitude where, on the second to the last day in May, the rain changes to snow. The lake was in a small bowl with steep-sided, thickly forested hills rising around it. The air and the water were still, and the slopes of the hills wandered in and out of the low clouds. The water was trout-cool, but the air was cooler, and steam rose from the lake. You couldn't ask for a prettier view, but you could sure ask for better weather to be out in.

We managed roughly four hours on the water, enough time to determine that the fishing was somewhere between very slow and dead. One small trout had been landed and another had been hooked briefly. The best guess was that those monstrous trout, inscrutable enough under normal conditions, were moping under the bottomed-out barometer.

(It's a little known fact that the barometer was actually invented by a fisherman. Its original purpose was not to measure atmospheric pressure, but to provide scientific-sounding excuses for not catching fish.)

I was the first one off the water, in spite of the fact that I hate to be the one to crap out while everyone else is still at it, even on a day when you have to stop to shake the snow off of your fly rod every few minutes. On the other hand, cold is cold, and when you're not catching fish there isn't much else to think about.

I hadn't given up on the idea of sticking it out—a lake like this can take more patience than skill to crack—but I wanted to stick it out next to a little campfire, so I walked into the woods looking for something resembling dry wood. I walked out of sight of the lake into a thick stand of spruce, but the old trick of finding dry, dead branches low down on the trunks was clearly not going to work. The snow fell on the top of the forest and then percolated down to fall as rain under what would normally be the "cover" of the trees. The pattering of water on the pine needles was the only sound.

I was wet, cold, miserable, and fishless, but, oddly enough, I now recall it all as being very beautiful.

Right about then I was struck with a serious case of bearanoia. If you've never had bearanoia, it's difficult to describe. Often you don't see, hear, or smell anything even mildly suspicious, but are nonetheless struck by the unreasoning certainty that you are about to be killed and eaten by a 1500-pound, drooling, carniverous animal. A half-pint of adrenaline enters your cerebral cortex, and that's hard to describe, too.

You want to run, but something also tells you you're not *supposed* to run. Then you realize you can't run because your legs don't work, and it's pretty much over. There you are in this lovely, misty, dripping, primeval-looking coniferous forest, one of the prettiest places you can remember seeing, trying not to mess your pants.

In a few more seconds it's gone, and you are left with only a vague, uneasy feeling that you don't belong there, that you are, in fact, trespassing.

With the gods as my witness, I will never tell another bear story in a bar again, nor will I ever drink another jumper cable.

There may have been some dry wood back in there somewhere, but I returned to the lake with a hastily gathered armload of rubbery, dripping twigs that would not start, even with the help of the sports page from the local newspaper. When the boys saw what I was up to, they all paddled in to get warm and then stood around helplessly as the last pitiful whiffs of smoke vanished into the falling snow.

Someone said that although this might be considered a nice day in Oregon, "around here we get the hell out before we freeze to death."

And that's what we did.

The next morning we lingered over breakfast at the Corral Cafe as the snow, which had moved downhill overnight, began to stick in the parking lot. It was observed that it would be even colder at the lake today, and snowing harder; that maybe the dirt road to the trailhead was no longer passable; that the barometer was still low, and so on. We finally agreed that Rat Lake, with its big rainbow/cutthroat hybrids, might as well be on another planet, and that the best thing to do was pack up and go to Idaho where, we'd been told, it wasn't snowing nearly as hard.

The cafe was warm and cozy and smelled of good food. The log walls were covered with the obligatory skins, antlers, and stuffed heads. (You can see more wildlife in some of these joints than you would in a week in the backcountry.) Over the bar was a sign saying, "Caution, the Surgeon General has determined that bar tabs cause amnesia."

Ah, Montana, with its big rivers, big trout, log taverns, lonely cowboys, boyish fishing guides, pickup trucks, cats sleeping on pool tables, grizzly bears, straightforward sense of humor, and late snowstorms; where they watch the stream flows more closely than the stock market. As a place to drink coffee and figure out what to do next, it's better than most.

As we walked out to the truck with Idaho on our minds, someone asked me, "Well, what are you gonna write about Rat Lake?" I said I didn't know, but that I'd think of something, and it occurred to me that writing and fishing are alike in at least three ways: both demand a degree of persistence, both can turn out differently than you'd planned, and both are worth doing for their own sakes, even if you don't get what you're after—that is, either fish or money.

It also occurred to me that my back didn't hurt anymore, or, if it did, it wasn't enough to worry about. Just the normal stiffness from uphill walking and belly boating in cold water. I was cured.

There must be a moral there somewhere.

Big Sky, Montana
1987

THE
BIG
EMPTY
RIVER

Last summer the notorious Charles K. (Koke) Winter bought it on the Henry's Fork in southern Idaho, by which I mean he took a fall and broke his leg. "A word of advice," he told me recently. "If you're ever walking along the banks of the Henry's Fork and a pair of sandhill cranes fly over, stop walking first, *then* look."

If Koke was going to break something while fishing (and anyone who knows him would have told you it was just waiting to happen), it's like him to do it on one of the most famous trout streams in the world. He has a way of doing things like that; of engineering even his accidents so that, in the retelling, they can't help but sound heroic.

He somehow managed to achieve a spiral fracture—the classic downhill skiing injury—and so naturally someone down at the health club asked him, in that snide way people have when you're hurt, "How's the skiing?"

"I don't go in for sissy sports," Koke answered, "I'm a trout fisherman."

That kind of style is something you have to be born with.

I've never broken anything on the Henry's Fork, not even a fly rod, but I've fished it every year since the first time I laid eyes on it. That puts me in the company of thousands of other fly-fishers from all over the country and even in the rest of the world—the people whose cars and trucks, during the Green Drake hatch at least, make that little patch of gravel in front of Mike Lawson's fly shop look like the parking lot at the United Nations building.

I first fished the river because it had become unavoidable. Everyone talked about it, quoted magazine articles about it, showed pictures of it, and even drove up there to fish in it now and then. More to the point, they all used it as a kind of measure against which all other trout streams were judged. A great rainbow trout was "like a Henry's Fork fish," a heavy mayfly hatch was "like you'd see on the Henry's Fork," a wide, slow section of any river was "just like the Fork above Osborn Bridge." I got the feeling they must have a 100-yard stretch of it on display at the Bureau of Standards as an example of *the* trout stream, right next to *the* foot, *the* pound, and so on. I finally had to go fish the thing just so I could hold up my end of the conversation.

That first trip was something of a turning point. It wasn't my first famous river, but it was my first truly mythological one. It was also the first time I fished with Koke and began to get an inkling of how famous *he* was. Everyone knew him and everyone who took the time to talk had a story, each one less believable than the last. Enormous trout, convoluted ethics, feats of strength and daring, elaborate practical jokes, and other things, too. Koke Winter stories could fill a book, and I hope they do someday. Of course, Koke will have to write it himself. No one else would dare to say half of it in print.

Some years later, while I was working in a fly shop in Boulder, Colorado, Koke came in doing his jerk act—asking about our live bait selection, referring to the fly rods as "crawler poles," and so on. It was clear to the other customers that we knew each other, so when he left someone asked, "Who the hell was that?"

"His name is Koke Winter," I said.

"*That* was Koke Winter!?" the man said. "Jeeze!" And then everyone gazed reverently at the empty spot where his car had been parked.

This was also the first long trip (the first of many) that I took with Archie (A.K.) Best. A.K. and I had been fishing together before, but it was the first Henry's Fork expedition that sealed us as partners.

A road trip can do that by getting all the cards on the table. It can also accomplish the opposite. The usual hardships of getting out early, getting in late, getting lost, getting rained on, getting skunked, and all the other things you can get tend to reveal character in a matter of days. Creeps and idiots cannot conceal themselves for long on a fishing trip.

A.K. and I have been all over hell together since then—mostly just the two of us, based on our shared perception that two fishermen are a partnership, while any more than that constitutes a committee. We now set up our camps with such wordless efficiency that spectators sometimes think we're mad at each other. I've learned a lot from him, from the nuts and bolts of fly tying and casting—both of which he's damned good at—to philosophy. It was while fishing with A.K. that I discovered you could tell the plain truth about fly-fishing and still be a humorist.

I've learned a lot from him even though he's never *taught* me a damned thing, and although this didn't exactly start on the Henry's Fork, it was there that it hit cruising speed.

The first time I saw the river my mind was boggled more than that of the normal pilgrim because of what Koke had done to us. Koke, A.K., a man named Tom Abbot, and I set out from Colorado in a borrowed camper: an enormous six-mile-to-the-gallon land yacht that, in a single two-week trip, soured me on these vehicles forever.

For one thing, it wouldn't go over forty-five mph, even across Wyoming where most drivers change flat tires at forty-five.

It ate gas as if it was still the 1950s.

It was supposed to "sleep six comfortably" but was actually about big enough for two or three close (and I mean *close*) friends with their gear and a change of clothes each. The fourth man was too many, and it was never quite clear who the fourth man was.

The thing was also furnished in late cafe gothic, so that even if you were parked in the middle of fabulous scenery, you felt like you were camped with a bunch of declining rock musicians in a sleazy motel on East Colfax Avenue in Denver.

And there was the unbearable suspense over whether the thing would start in the morning.

But the worst part was that it was slow. I've since learned that the drive to the Henry's Fork is a crisp twelve hours with six driving shifts between two people and as many piss, gas, and coffee stops. A breeze in a real road car or a serviceable pickup. Now I'm not the speed freak I once was—not like when Ed Engle and I would get off work at our landscaping jobs, hop in his car, blast from Boulder, Colorado, to Laramie, Wyoming, find a truck stop, order coffee, ask the waitress what state we were in and what the date was, and be back in time for work the next morning—but I do like to get where I'm going, and so does A.K.

In fact, A.K. gets downright kittenish about it sometimes. He's even been known to drag race occasionally when one of those rural hot rodders in the fifteen-foot-tall pickups, with the balloon tires, chrome stacks, and pinstriping revs his engine at us at a stoplight. A.K.'s pickup is rather hot, and he's been known to win, much to the dismay of several teenagers across the western United States.

You can never tell about those old guys in fishing hats.

So there we were, cooped up in this lumbering dinosaur, creeping across Wyoming, being passed by one little old lady in a Volkswagen after another. After about eighteen hours of that, you start to get a little testy.

Koke let that work on us all by itself until we came down off the pass into Idaho on the long-awaited last leg. Then he started. There were places where we had to stop and look at the scenery— and with Koke you don't just look, you speculate on the place's geologic history and determine which plants are edible and which are not. It can take an hour.

Then there was the final gas stop in Tetonia or Driggs (known as Dregs by the locals) or one of those other little towns that are an hour or so from the final destination. Koke had to tour all the gas stations to find the cheapest price, then he had to check the air in the tires, and the oil, and the water in the radiator—all of which were, of course, fine.

Then he had to have an ice cream cone. It took him fifteen

minutes to pick one out, and then he started with the clerk. "Tell me, sir, is this ice cream 'quiescently frozen?'"

We had to stop to look at a single trumpeter swan in a puddle by the side of the highway, which I'd have been happy to do at any other time, except that by then we were twelve miles from the Henry's Fork for Christ's sake! Gimme a break, Koke.

When we finally arrived at the river, three of us exploded from the camper, hit the water running with fly rods still unstrung and wader suspenders unfastened, and proceeded to fall in, not catch fish, and otherwise make fools of ourselves, while Koke sat quietly on the back step of the camper and calmly took forty-five minutes to tie up the perfect leader, smiling to himself all the time.

The bastard.

In seasons since I have come to learn that Koke's sense of humor is among the most dangerous in existence, because it's practiced for his own amusement alone. It doesn't matter if you get it or not. In fact, it's probably better if you don't. And the funniest thing imaginable to him is to shake your composure while retaining his.

All that notwithstanding, there it was: the fabled Henry's Fork, and in the last week in June, too, at the height of the Green Drake mayfly hatch. In all of human experience there are only four metaphysical summits: Valhalla, Heaven, Nirvana, and the Green Drake hatch on the Henry's Fork.

The Henry's Fork is known as the river where insect hatches come off not only heavily, but regularly, "like clockwork." That's probably close to true, but it would be more accurate to say they come off *more* like clockwork there than on most other streams. There are glitches even in paradise.

For instance, there was a season in recent memory when the Green Drakes didn't come off at all, for reasons that may never be reliably determined. It just didn't happen. Another year the hatch came off just fine, but a million sea gulls arrived and ate most of them. They didn't eat all of them, of course, but even though there were still some bugs on the water, the swooping, diving gulls spooked the trout and the fishing was lousy. I missed that year, but I understand several thousand fly-fishers were seriously bummed out.

Relative to that season, I once overheard the following conversation in the A-Bar on the banks of the Fork at Last Chance, Idaho:

First fisherman (obviously inebriated and a bit sentimental): "You remember the year the sea gulls mucked up the hatch?"

Second fisherman: "Yeah."

First fisherman, after a long pause: "You know, life is like that."

Second fisherman: "Like fishing?"

First fisherman: "No, like sea gulls."

The point is, if it happened on the Henry's Fork, it was profound.

The Henry's Fork is the favorite trout stream of so many fly-fishers because it's exactly what you'd dream up for yourself if you could invent the perfect place using only thin air and the loftiest elements of the fly-fishing tradition. It's big and sprawling—some say it's the largest legitimate spring creek in the world—and it's not fast and brawling like many western rivers. It is, in fact, a sedate, quiet river, at least below Box Canyon. In most places the wading is between easy and effortless, and it's been described as like a flooded parking lot. I'll buy that if you take that parking lot and scatter a few tripping-sized boulders and some surprise holes around in it. There are a few places where the wading fisherman can't go, but there are damned few he can't at least reach.

And that's a good thing because the trout are everywhere. Sure, some spots are better than others, but most of the river bottom is matted with thick vegetation which is, in turn, grazed upon by a staggering number of aquatic nymphs that periodically emerge to become some of the most famous hatches in the literature of the sport. There are the real glamor bugs: the Green, Brown, and Gray Drakes, Blue-winged Olives, Pale Morning Duns, Callibaetis (Speckled Duns), tiny Black & White Trikes, Mahogany Duns, and others. There are also the spotty and mysterious flying ant falls, the bankside ants, beetles, and hoppers, and, of course, the workmanlike caddis hatches, which can be as delicately technical as any of the supposedly classier mayflies.

If you catch any of these bugs at their best on the Henry's Fork, it will be "the heaviest (fill in the blank) hatch I've ever seen," and you will babble on about it for weeks afterwards to anyone who will listen.

The trout, mostly rainbows, are large, fat, healthy, and hard fighting, and they continue to feed on insects even when they've grown well past the 20-inch mark. That, one assumes, is because there are so many bugs and so many slow currents where the fish don't have to work their little tails off to get at them.

As if the river wasn't pretty enough, it meanders through sweepingly beautiful Idaho country that is stalked by everything from sandhill cranes (stop walking, *then* look) to moose.

Given the power, this is what you'd create for yourself, but, because you're not dumb or lazy, you'd also include a few whitefish so you'd have to learn to tell the difference between their rises and those of the trout; you'd make the rainbows maddeningly picky about fly patterns and presentation to keep things interesting; and you'd include a mechanism by which the hatches were predictably regular, but still moody, so that even working from the hatch chart in the back of Mike Lawson's catalog, it would still be possible to miss them.

It would be perfect, if you agree that perfection must include the dramatic element of chance, or, put another way, the possibility of failure.

You probably wouldn't include the crowds, however. In my own fantasy, the river is owned by me, the way Averell Harriman once owned the Railroad Ranch stretch, except that my guests wouldn't be magnates and diplomats. They'd be a ratty congregation of fly-fishers who would stay for months, camped next to their pickups at discreet distances from one another, now and then coming to the lodge to use the shower. If I didn't want my ducks and moose eaten, I'd have to check firearms at the front gate.

Okay, back to reality.

The first time I fished the Fork, and a number of times thereafter, I was as intimidated by the crowd as by the river itself.

There was neoprene, Gore-Tex, and graphite from horizon to horizon, punctuated by the occasional spot of rubberized canvas and the odd wheat-colored gleam of split cane. During the Green Drake hatch, one of the most heavily attended events in fly-fishing, there are literally hundreds of fishermen on the water on any given day. And many of them are very good. Last summer, Mike Lawson told me, "Not only are there more fishermen on the river now than there were ten years ago, there are a lot more *good* fishermen."

It *is* the kind of place where experts gather and the competition—if you care to engage in it—can be wilting. It can be quite the fashionable scene, and there seem to be a few hotshots who travel all the way to Idaho every year just to hold court; to stand around on the bank with their entourage offering critiques of their colleagues' casting styles and fishing tactics. Now and then you'll actually see one of these guys fishing.

Of course, the people are all fly-fishers and, therefore, mostly nice guys, but the sheer numbers can be daunting. You can get into them on a one-to-one basis, though: you meet someone, exchange the usual news and pleasantries, and in a matter of minutes you're pals, complaining about the crowd as if you weren't both part of it.

Ultimately, if you're going to fish the Green Drake hatch, you have to accept and even come to enjoy the people, otherwise the fishing will be a chore, no matter how good it is. This is, after all, a hastily assembled subculture, and as such it's not a bad one. For one thing, values are unquestioned: mayflies and rising trout are good, wind and sea gulls are bad, period. By being even mildly sociable, you can learn a lot about insects (in both English and Latin), fly patterns, fish behavior, casting, stalking . . . In fact, if you don't come to think of yourself as "something of a fly-fisherman" and start making snide remarks from the safety of shore, you can learn more in a week than you can in a whole winter of reading.

Even on that first trip, however, I learned that there are ways of fishing the Henry's Fork in relative solitude. We'd come for the same reason everyone else had—for the Green Drakes—and it was actually just fine. The big mayflies would begin to come off at about ten in the morning and continue sporadically until about three in the afternoon.

Naturally, the bugs themselves were fantastic: big, grayish-olive, long-winged flies that, as the legend says, lured even the largest of the trout to the surface where they could be hooked on dry flies. Some angling myths are actually true, and this is one of them.

Considering that the trout were spoiled, bored, spring creek fish, they rose greedily, but, as in most situations like this, no one was hauling them in hand over fist. Both the fly pattern and its presentation had to be close to perfect, and even then it wasn't a lock. Even the steadily rising fish would let a few naturals go by now and then, out of spite.

It took a good eye, too. Those of us with little previous experience with the mountain whitefish often wasted a good deal of time casting carefully to these much-disliked nontrouts. White-fish are edible, and native, but they're still the fool's trout; like fool's gold they can be the source of some disappointment and considerable embarrassment. They're also sometimes known as "turd knockers."

If there's one secret to fishing the Henry's Fork (there are actually many secrets), it's the downstream drift. My first impression of the Green Drake water across from Lawson's was, "These people are all fishing backwards," but an hour later I was doing it myself because it was the only way to get a good, long, drag-free float in all those conflicting currents.

That year the hot fly was the big green Paradrake, as designed by Messrs. Swisher and Richards and as tied by the thousands somewhere in the Third World. It's a complicated fly with a dyed elk-hair body—complete with extended abdomen and tails—an upright hair wing and parachute hackle. It was a fly none of us had with us and one I still can't tie so it *stays* tied for more than a few minutes.

When we pulled in that first day, we went over to Lawson's shop to get The Word. The Word on events like this is usually brief and somewhat simplified for mass consumption, but still useful, generally consisting of hatch times and patterns.

We'd no sooner walked through the door when a man burst in behind us. He held a strung-up fly rod with a dangling, flyless leader, his waders were dripping Henry's Fork spring water on the carpet, and his eyes were big and glazed. He dashed to the counter and dipped his hand into the large fishbowl that held hundreds of loose Paradrakes, dumping about a dozen of them on the counter along with a fifty-dollar bill. And then he was out the door, heading back toward the river in the waddling trot peculiar to men in baggy waders.

"That must be the pattern," I said to Mike.

"Yup," he answered.

I bought a half-dozen and so did A.K., but it was harder on him. To A.K., fly-fishing involves catching fish with a split bamboo fly rod using flies you've tied yourself. It's something between a matter of pride and an esthetic judgement. Don't get me wrong. He doesn't care what *you* do. In fact, he's a professional flytier and would starve if the majority of fishermen didn't buy at least some of the flies they fish with.

Still, as he peeled some bills from a modest roll and handed them over, he announced, "I've tied twenty-five-hundred-dozen flies this year and it burns my ass to have to buy these!" The assembled customers stopped talking and looked up for a moment— but only for a moment. Fishermen get used to the occasional emotional outburst.

In case you don't have your calculator handy, that's 30,000 individual flies.

There are, naturally, other drake patterns. There's the Green Drake Wulff, Mike's extended body Green Drake, and the pretty Harrop Green Drake, not to mention various hackle tip-winged flies, a number of emerger patterns, the Iwamasa Dun, and, of course, the size 10 Adams. (Apparently there are a number of very proficient, mostly local Henry's Fork fly-fishers—born-again presentationists—who use nothing but the Adams dry fly in sizes 10 through 24 on all of the river's confusing hatches and who catch more fish than anyone has a right to.)

In the end, it's a matter of personal style as practiced by people who have given it a lot of thought. This is why you can hear heated discussions between two flytiers—both of whom are catching fish—about the "correct" color of the Drake.

"It's a yellowish, olivish, tan with a hint of pale dun."

"Are you blind? It's a tannish olive with a hint of pale yellow."

It was fine, not unlike attending a convention, but then one evening Koke suggested we go to a place he knew about downstream to see if the Brown Drakes were hatching. "There may not be as many people," he said.

We walked in to a stretch of river so slow flowing it was almost glassy. I've since learned that all the regulation bugs hatch there and are eaten by trout, but it's prime Brown Drake water because its bottom is silty and the Brown Drake nymph is a burrower, rather than a rock clinger.

I'd never seen the Brown Drake mayfly before, but I'd heard of it, and all the stories were true. It's a huge bug as mayflies go and, although they hatch in the low light of dusk, you can clearly see them sitting on the water at fifty yards. They look like sailboats.

I know that comparison has been overused, but that's what they look like. It's not my fault.

Once the hatch has been going on for a night or two, there's also a simultaneous spinner fall. All at the same time, there are nymphs rising from the bottom, emergers at the surface, hatched duns *on* the surface, and last night's bugs, molted into their sexually mature form, mating in the air, laying their eggs on the water and dying. And the trout are eating all of them.

If it wasn't for that last part—the part about the trout eating up the bugs—a guy could probably get all misty and reverent about this great orgy of birth, death, and rebirth; but these are really big trout. Sympathy for the insects is not the emotion that comes immediately to mind.

It sounds great—and it is—but it's also something of a problem because the trout get selective to one particular stage. And not *the trout* as a group, but each individual fish. You want to fish the dun pattern because the bug itself is so handsome, with its brownish body and wings mottled like the breast feathers of a grouse, but then there's a bigger fish eating the emergers, and, once you've switched to that pattern, an even bigger one sipping the spinners. The hatch can last for an hour or two and it's possible to spend that entire time changing from one fly to another and then back to the one you started with. Believe me.

The next day I bought some Brown Drake flies at Lawson's. I found them not in a fishbowl on the counter but in a modest bin with all the rest of the flies; a few dozen rather than hundreds. The way the flies were displayed in the shop was a perfect model of the rate of fishing pressure on the two hatches.

We fished the Brown Drakes for several evenings running, during which time I learned that you settle on a certain pattern— say, the spinner—and try it over one fish after another until you find the one who wants spinners. If nothing else, it keeps you fishing instead of changing flies. I caught a fish or two, but that's not what I remember so well. What I remember is the loneliness and the quiet.

We weren't exactly alone there, but we were part of a manageable number of fishermen. There was enough for everyone and there were owls moving soundlessly through the trees and sandhill cranes making that chilling, prehistoric clatter. One night there was a crashing back in the woods. A moose, probably, but in that country there's always the possibility of grizzly bear.

In years since, in the evenings after other Green Drake hatches, A.K. and I have gone downstream to fish until past dark. We've never hit the big Brown Drakes again, but we will. We both carry boxes of the flies.

What we have found are the spinners of the Pale Morning Duns, and sometimes caddis. We've never caught a lot of fish there at night, but we've caught some big ones and have seen some even bigger.

It has never been crowded, and I don't know why. It might be the darkness. It's surprising how many fishermen, and very serious ones, too, will just not go out at night. I won't say I don't understand that because I now and then get spooked myself, but it usually turns out to have been worth it.

Once, on the Henry's Fork, I had stayed out later than everyone else. I didn't catch the fish I was after, and he finally stopped rising, so I struck out across a meadow toward the road and the truck where my partners were waiting.

Somewhere out there I stepped on a pair of nesting cranes. Two of them. Four feet tall. I screamed bloody murder, fell on my back, and lay there for five minutes trying to let it sink in that I wasn't dead, it was okay, it was just dark, that was all. Back at the truck someone said, "Heard you yell. Thought you were eaten by a bear. We were just gonna divide up your stuff."

But then some nights you *do* catch the fish, and it's incomparable. Reaching out into the dark river and feeling that tugging from what seems like another dimension is too eerie to describe. It must be experienced. Hooking a big trout at night seems like something that can't be done, but you just did it. For some reason, though, most don't even care to try it, and those who do night-fish don't seem to talk about it much.

What clouds the Henry's Fork in late June and early July isn't so much the Green Drake hatch, although that's a heavy calling card that draws fishermen from all over. What kills it is being the only game in town. Later in the year people scatter to other places: the Madison River, the Yellowstone, Hebgen Lake, and so on. That golden triangle where Idaho, Montana, and Wyoming all come together at Yellowstone Park is where you go when you die if you've been a good boy. It's got everything a fly-fisher could want, including the Henry's Fork, which has its best hatch when most everything else in the way of running water is slow.

Did I say *best* hatch? Let's change that to read "most well-known hatch." The best hatch I've fished so far on the Fork is the Callibaetis mayfly in the middle two weeks of August, which is known, for reasons that are beyond me, as the depths of the off season on that river.

Actually, you're not looking for the hatch at all, but the

spinner fall. The duns emerge sporadically, while the spinners fall all together, thousands of them, starting around nine or ten in the morning downstream from Last Chance, in the quietest water.

A.K. and I spent the better part of two weeks there last season with only the occasional side trip up to the Yellowstone River for cutthroats and Hebgen Lake for the "gulpers," big trout who are also eating—loudly—Callibaetis spinners. We stayed in the KOA Campground at Last Chance so long the manager finally asked us to move our tent to another spot. Seems we were killing the grass.

We'd arise around dawn, A.K. happy and energetic, me not *un*happy, but much slower, bolt coffee and breakfast, stop at the cafe for a couple of enormous cinnamon rolls fresh from the oven for lunch, and hit the water a good hour and a half before the hatch.

The first morning we were there early out of enthusiasm and because even the best hatch charts show only average or ideal times and dates. Good thing. If we'd come later, we'd have missed all but the tail end of the little black & white duns. We'd have also missed the young bull moose we spotted several times, always early in the morning, and came to refer to as Bullwinkle. A full grown bull moose is as stately and handsome an animal as any walking the planet, but a young bull, with his little antlers and enormous nose, is, well . . . cute.

The Callibaetis fall would come off more or less on schedule, and last for anywhere from two to four hours. The larger trout seemed ambivalent about the little black & whites, but they were *on* the Callibaetis from the word go. They'd start rising before you noticed the bugs on the water.

The fishing was difficult or, as they say now, "highly technical." The current was slow and smooth, the water was clear, the bugs were small (about a size 16), and the fish were Henry's Fork rainbows who will literally count the number of tails on a mayfly before eating it in slow water like this where they have the time.

The fish were also cruisers, which Mike says is something we fishermen taught them to do. Years ago you could find big rainbows lying in one spot in the current sipping bug after bug. These fish were not always easy to catch, but you could at least show them your fly and be fairly sure they'd seen it.

Mike has seen the change in his years on the river. Now the larger trout will pick a good stretch of current and move up through it lazily, taking a bug here, a bug there, and then one over there, seldom rising in the same place twice in a row. Until you figure it out, it can look like six or eight enormous trout all rising sporadically instead of what it is: one big fish passing through.

It gets more complicated. Sometimes it *is* six or eight fish, and they're all passing through at their own speed, some fast, some slow. Sometimes they seem to work up twenty or thirty yards of stream, then drift back down and do it again. In the slowest water, they'll sometimes noodle around in an area no larger than a small motel room, again, never coming up twice in the same spot.

The worst is the huge trout who works up past you and just keeps going, never to be seen again. You get two or three casts to him, and then you're standing there like you were late for your own wedding and just missed the last bus.

On the other hand, you'll now and then find one who actually *does* stay in one place. In fact, this may be the reason why so many fishermen in recent years have come to love the bank feeders on the Fork. They're just as hard to catch, but at least they'll stay put.

This can rattle you out of the traditional slow, contemplative pace of fine dry-fly-fishing, but don't let it. As tempting as it is, you won't catch fish by chasing them—at least not very many. It sounds paradoxical, but the way to deal with cruising trout in this situation is to take the pace even slower than usual.

And don't be greedy, either. I've watched many a very good fly-fisher work this slow water and have never seen anyone take more than a few fish in a single session. The trout are hard; many of them are quite big. If you get a few fish in a day, maybe even a 20-incher or better, you've done as well as anyone deserves to do. As A.K. says, the slow water on the Henry's Fork is where you go when you've already caught enough fish to prove whatever it was you had to prove. Now you want to see how good your nerves are.

On that trip, fishing the same spinner fall morning after morning, A.K. and I both landed several 20-inch (or slightly better) trout and hooked and lost at least as many more, if you agree that any trout who takes you into the backing and breaks you off was, "at least 20 inches," even if he was only 16.

I'm especially proud of one of mine because I worked on him for three mornings and hooked and lost him twice before finally landing him. He was one of those rare trout who actually stay in one place, in this case, probably because it was such a difficult spot to cast to that he felt secure.

He was one of those unperturbable trout. I'd make a bad cast and he'd go down, but I'd keep my eye on the place and in fifteen minutes or so he'd be back, rising steadily. So *I'd* go back and maybe hook him this time, but get broken off. That would be it for the day, but the next morning, there he'd be, sipping the same flies in the same place again.

Given the time—days, weeks—you will sooner or later catch a fish like this. And you take the time. It can become very important.

On two separate days, the Callibaetis were followed by a good fall of flying ants. Actually, the ants came toward the end of the spinner fall, but they must have been delicious, because every fish in the river switched to them immediately. The first day I didn't have anything in the box that was even close, though I did manage to tempt one nice rainbow with a surgically altered Humpy. That afternoon in camp I tied up a dozen reasonable copies, and so did A.K., who had had two when the fall came on, had lost one, and was not about to go back the next day with a single fly.

As we finished tying, A.K. said, "Well, that takes care of the (deleted) ants," an allusion to Murphy's Law of matching the hatch, which says that tying a good supply of flies to copy an unexpected hatch insures that said hatch will not come off again until you are out of the state.

But, wonder of wonders, it did come off, four days later. Mike had told us the ants were one of the most enigmatic events on the river. "You can fish for a month and not hit it," he said. "You guys were lucky." And that was referring to the first time.

The trout took those ants with as much enthusiasm as I've ever seen Henry's Fork fish exhibit. We caught a bunch, maybe a dozen between us in less than an hour. There have been years when we didn't take a dozen fish in that stretch in two weeks and thought *that* was great.

And that's not even the best part. The best part is, on the entire trip, in the half-mile or so of river that interests us most, we saw as many moose as we did other fishermen. Three each.

On the drive home I said that this had been the season on the Henry's Fork that I'd been paying my dues for all these years, but it was A.K. (as usual) who summed it up properly. The afternoon of the second ant fall as we hiked back to the truck literally whipped from day after day of catching big trout, he said, making the quotation marks in the air with his fingers, "Well, that'll teach us to come in the 'off season.'"

The Henry's Fork is one of those rivers that has been written about and photographed unmercifully. If cameras really did steal souls, the place would be a field by now. It also constitutes one of the great paradoxes in outdoor writing. Editors will say they're sorry, but they just don't need "yet another story on the Henry's Fork." Then, a few months later, yet another story on the Henry's Fork appears in that very magazine. We—readers, writers, and editors alike—just can't leave it alone and are now, in fact, in the final stages of loving it to death. It's not surprising, since Last Chance, Idaho, is, and will probably remain, the spiritual center of the Rocky Mountains. When you pull up to it in your camper, you haven't just gotten there, you have *arrived*. Even to those who fish it regularly, it is "The Henry's Fork," as much an idea as a trout stream. To the rest of us, it's Mecca.

As fed up as I sometimes get with the crowds, I also have to say that, if you love, or even just like, trout rivers, *you have got to see this one*. And once you see it you have to stay long enough or come back often enough to solve at least one or two of its many puzzles. After all, this is not a spectator sport we're talking about.

In all fairness, it might be time for those of us who have fished it some to write our little memoirs and then move on to the Falls, or the Teton or the Bitterroot or one of the other less pounded rivers this part of the world offers, leaving the fabled Fork to the many newcomers who are currently making fly-fishing a "growth industry."

I don't know if I'll be able to do that or not, but it will help to consider that what many of us love about this place is now at least partly an illusion. The photos of the Fork you see in magazines and catalogs typically show one, or at most two, fishermen standing in the otherwise vacant river—blissful loneliness, man and the wilderness and all that. These stark compositions can be hard to come by at times, what with all the people standing around, but, like the big fish, given the time you can get one. The camera doesn't lie, but it can pick its moments.

This, I think, is an acceptable use of poetic license—acceptable because that's how we want to see the place. Crowded or not, it is still the Big, Empty River.

THE
FEATURELESS
DISK

This is not a smokescreen. I honestly don't know the name of the lake, and I'm not sure if that was cleverly engineered by my host or just an oversight on my part. As I recall, it just never came up. I do, however, remember exactly how to get there.

This is the smokescreen: It's somewhere in northern Wyoming.

Jay Allman of Trout Traps, Ltd.—the belly boat makers—called me up one spring day to ask if I'd like to go to Wyoming to fish for some very big rainbow trout in a small lake, the classic float tube situation. Silly question.

It was to be one of those breakneck trips: drive up one day, fish for two, and haul back the fourth, switching drivers every hundred miles, swilling roadhouse coffee and trying to stay awake. I hesitated for a full minute only because of the ratio between fishing and windshield time (I like it to be better than half and half on the fishing side) but the fact is, if you wave a big fish in front of me I'll go, and at pretty short notice, too. I mean, what else do I have to do? Make a living? "I'll just work twice as hard when I get back," I tell myself; the battle cry of the self-employed. A good friend who just last week lured me away from what is supposedly my life's work said, "Gierach, you're so easy. It's a good thing for you you're not a girl."

The clincher, if a clincher was needed, was that we'd be guided
for nothing, all we had to do was get there.

We got there in Jay's new, silver Jeep-style station wagon with
the stereo tape deck and a good collection of rock and roll: an
admirably tight-steering, music-blasting road car. There was even
room for fishermen, gear, and an armada of float tubes.

The actual trip is now a blur. We drove almost the whole
way across Wyoming, south to north, and all I clearly remember
is stopping in Chugwater for gas. Chugwater sounds made up,
but it's a real town; one on the same level of obscurity as Wam-
sutter (which is sometimes referred to as Whumpsucker, Stump-
knocker, and so on). Both are small, dusty, and quaint and will
probably appear on one of Charles Kuralt's "On the Road" spots
if they haven't already. If you're ever in Chugwater, stop at the
gas station and check out the owner's fabulous collection of
baseball caps.

The blur cleared as we met our guide, Willie Strausheim—also
known to friends and clients as Wyoming Willie—had a good
steak dinner, and something approaching a night's sleep. I sometimes sleep poorly the first few nights on the road, and the
inherent drama of a 4:30 wakeup call didn't help.

We were on the lake a little past dawn the following morning,
and the memory suddenly becomes sharp.

It was the perfect size; small but not so small as to be what
you'd call "intimate." It was bigger than what people call a pond, but
not much bigger. You couldn't shout across it and be understood,
but you could be heard. It was not exactly hidden, but it was twice
removed from the main county highway and invisible until you
were almost on it. There was no sign hinting at its presence, even
at the last turnoff. This was public water, but not public knowledge,
and Willie said something I've heard a time or two before. "Feel
free to write about this, but please don't say where it is."

That's always a reasonable request, and I honor it with the
steadfastness some reserve for things like wedding vows. Not only
is it the honorable thing to do, but an outdoor writer who gets
a reputation as a kiss-and-tell fisherman sooner or later finds
himself fishing alone.

This was the archetypal prairie lake: at a high enough altitude and cold enough to hold trout, but low enough and warm enough to be rich in vegetation and bugs. Lakes like this are seldom seen on the covers of outdoor magazines because they're less than wildly scenic. In fact, they're often very ordinary-looking, lying among low hills covered with rough grass and grazing cattle. The cows actually contribute to the richness of the water as the nutrients from their "agricultural by-products," otherwise known as meadow muffins, leech into the lake. Unlike streams, trout lakes don't usually have cutbanks that are ruined by cattle, and the cattle don't seem to hurt anything else, but they're not elk or deer, so magazine art directors don't like them.

The air was warm for spring, and calm, and the sun was bright. Not the best fishing weather. You want a chop on the surface, a light rain, or at least overcast skies to make the fish feel safer about cruising into the shallows to feed. As we rigged up, a few trout rose lazily here and there in random spots. Not bunched in one area or in a band off shore, but genuinely *here and there*.

I've fished a lot of these prairie trout lakes and I dearly love them, but there's still a feeling of emptiness in my stomach when I see one. It seems like a featureless disk with no points of reference, a smooth surface occasionally broken by a rising trout, but with no fish-attracting structures and no apparent logic. It usually passes, this feeling, but it's always been a large part of fishing for me; overcoming the helplessness.

There are still a lot of fly-fishermen around who don't like lakes, and some of that sentiment is legitimate. Too many fair-to-middling trout lakes now sit over what were once very *good* trout streams that were dammed up so lawns could be watered and toilets could be flushed a hundred miles away.

Toilets? Okay, I'll give you toilets, but if you move out here to the high plains of the West and expect to have a Marion Blue-grass lawn like you had in Ohio, you're not getting into the spirit of things. This is the last quarter of the twentieth century; we're not Puritans conquering the wilderness now, we're marginally enlightened humans trying to live our lives and still leave the place inhabitable. Bluegrass is not supposed to grow out here. What grows here is yucca and prickly pear and scrub oak and such, none of which has to be watered. Or mowed.

End of editorial.

Many of the prairie lakes are man-made empoundments, but I don't mind them too much because of where they are. Many are out on the flatlands where trout habitat begins to get questionable, and in a nice, coincidental way, they can make the last of that trout water about as good as it can get and also spread it out so there's more of it. Granted, it's not a river anymore—at least for a stretch—but there can be enormous trout there, and you can't just turn your back on that, can you?

Ecological concerns aside, some fly-fishers dislike lakes because the water doesn't go anywhere. It just *sits* there. In a stream or river, the water moves. It undercuts banks, it piles up log jams, it eddies behind rocks and flattens out in pools. If you know that trout like edges—most notably the places where fast, aerated, food-carrying water becomes slow, easy-to-lie-in water—the places where the fish will be become almost self-evident.

Okay, maybe that's a little rash. Let's say the places where they *should* be can be evident, and sometimes they're actually there. We talk about "reading water," and it's a good analogy as long as you realize it's more like reading a novel than like the directions on a box of pancake mix. Meaning piles up in layers, and the truth that's revealed can't be distilled out into anything simpler than the whole thing.

Some lakes can be read like streams. Give me a shallow, sloping, weedy shelf with a dropoff at the edge in an otherwise rocky-bottomed lake, and I'll tell you where the trout are supposed to be. And sooner or later they'll be there, too. If not right now, then come evening, or maybe next morning. Of course, a good hatch or fall of insects will make the trout rise, and then it's as easy as it was difficult before. Rising trout *are* like the directions on a box of pancake mix, only simpler:

Step 1: The trout are right there, see?

It doesn't mean you'll catch them, but you don't have to wonder where the hell they are.

But the prairie lakes are sometimes all but impossible to

decipher. Their bottoms are uniformly dish-shaped and often just as uniformly covered with aquatic vegetation. The insects and other food organisms have certain preferences, but bugs in general are pretty much evenly distributed. Some lakes seem to specialize in certain fish foods, like freshwater shrimp, for instance, while others hold an incredible diversity.

A little bottom kicking showed that Wyoming Willie's lake held the usual trout stream things: mayflies, midges, caddis flies, shrimp, crane flies (with the expected absence of stoneflies, which need colder water and more aeration), plus some stuff usually associated with warmer water like damselflies, dragonflies, backswimmer beetles, aquatic beetle larvae, leeches, salamanders, tadpoles, and well, I got tired of looking.

These conditions can grow breathtakingly big trout, which is the attraction, but those fish can be just about anywhere with no apparent rhyme or reason. The lake bottom is just more pasture land, like you see on the surrounding hills, and the trout often behave like the cows do. The cattle will be scattered around randomly because anyplace is as good as any other place, and that's where the trout will be: anyplace. Trout move a little faster than cows, and, being predatory, they're a bit more aggressive. They're prettier, but no smarter.

Wyoming Willie cops to this in his fishing. During midday when the fish are scattered, he trolls from his belly boat, making lazy ellipses and figure-eights covering roughly one-quarter of the lake at a time. There's a touch to this, and it's a light one. He uses a long, fairly fine leader and a nymph that rides just inches below the surface, and he goes *very* slowly. When you glance over at him, he doesn't seem to be moving at all, but he's always in a slightly different place. Like the cows on the hillside.

He also moves the rod tip slowly and gently from side to side, making the fly swim in a serpentine course and, by design, keeping it out of the water he's just paddled through at least 50 percent of the time. Good idea.

And then there's that series of incredibly subtle twitches of the line, timed to some mysterious personal vision of the fly in the water and the mind of the fish. All good fishermen have such a vision.

Willie is very good at this; I am not. Maybe I lack the patience or, more likely, the understanding of exactly how it works. I trolled from the belly boat some and even caught a few fish that way, but mostly I looked for risers.

The gospel on rising trout in lakes is this: The water stands still and the fish move. You have to cast ahead of them, after, of course, figuring out which way "ahead" is, which is not always easy.

Fine, but in the prairie lakes it doesn't always work. During hatches, or in the presence of windblown shoals of floating insects or other concentrations of bugs, these big, lazy, self-satisfied trout will sometimes just wallow around in one spot, not moving because they don't have to.

I actually remember the very day and the very fish I figured this out on. Gary LaFontaine and I were fishing one of the great prairie lakes on the Blackfeet Indian reservation in Northern Montana. It was the end of May—cold, blustery, nasty, wet—and we'd been told we were there too late. "The weather ain't bad enough," they said.

Too late or not, we did get some fish, and some big ones, too, but only when the Callibaetis mayflies were hatching. During one such hatch at Kipp's Lake, a big trout boiled out in front of me; one of those rolling boils that doesn't show enough fish to tell you which way he's going. Taking a guess, I cast to his right about five feet, let the lightly weighted nymph sink for a few seconds, and then began a slow retrieve.

In the previous days I had determined that the answer was the small Callibaetis nymph, the one with the ostrich herl along the abdomen to mimic the gills. It's what I was catching my few fish on. Gary, incidentally, had determined the answer to be the dry fly and that's how he was catching his. There was a time when things like that were great mysteries to me, but lately it's become clear: he got them on dry flies because that's how he wanted to do it.

So, I cast to the right and nothing happened. The fish boiled again and I cast to his left. Also nothing. This went on until that maddeningly reasonable internal voice spoke up. "Now, let's stop and look at this for a minute," it said. "We've been casting to either side of that fish for five minutes, but the fish hasn't moved an inch, has it? What should that tell us?"

This voice always seems to sound like my second-grade teacher, Mrs. Ford, who, as far as I know, never fished.

It was a hen rainbow weighing 8 pounds, and I hooked her on the first cast right to the boil.

A year later, on Spinney Mountain reservoir in Colorado, the fish were doing the same thing, and I spent half an hour leading one rise after another until I realized the fish weren't going anywhere. This is why you have to watch out for firmly held beliefs, especially those that can be chanted in neat little phrases like, "cast ahead of them." Beliefs can make evidence transparent.

I finally cast right to the fish and caught it.

"I thought we all learned this *last* time," said Mrs. Ford.

Something else interesting happened that day at Spinney. It was glorious early spring fishing weather—sooty clouds, wind, rain—and we were catching fish by casting directly to the boils and rises. Then A.K. asked, "Have you been getting all your fish over those dark spots out there?"

Dark spots?

Sure enough, there were oval shapes of different sizes that were just a little deeper brownish olive than the surrounding bottom. Weed beds. It hadn't been more than a few weeks since the ice, breaking up, had scoured this windward side of the lake, scraping away much of the weed growth, but leaving patches. The bugs were in the patches and the trout were eating the bugs. Simple—once you see it—and something else to remember.

Spinney is a great prairie lake, although I was told by a Division of Wildlife biologist that it doesn't come strictly under that definition because it's at too high an altitude. "It's a 'mountain park reservoir'," he said

"What's the difference?" I asked.

"Just where it is," he answered.

Spinney is a classic example of the new reservoir syndrome that can make the first few years in the life of a freshly filled empoundment its best. It was once gently sloping pasture land with the South Platte River flowing through it. When all that formerly dry land was flooded, the cow pies and plants began to pump unusual nutrient levels into the water. The rich water grew an unusual amount of aquatic vegetation, which fed an unusual number of aquatic insects and forage fish which, in their turn, fed the trout that were stocked there. Those trout achieved a growth rate that was—all together now—unusual.

They stocked browns and cutthroats, a nice mix that gives you spawning runs up the stream inlet both spring and fall, and those fish began to grow like there was no tomorrow. Soon 4- and 5-pounders were the norm. As you'd expect, anglers of all persuasions arrived in flocks, droves, herds, gaggles, or whatever you'd call a large congregation of fishermen. In this day and age, we should have a word for that. Any suggestions?

The population of large fish in a new reservoir will increase for a number of years, the fishing will get better and better, traffic will increase, the nearest little gas, worms, and cold beer store will run out of bait, booze, and sandwiches, and it will be touted in and out of print as the "hot spot," "the best lake in the state." The next record such-and-such is expected to be hauled out at any moment.

During what may have been Spinney Mountain's height, I talked to a local accomplished float tuber who said he and his partners were regularly taking cutthroats weighing 7 and 8 pounds, but, "They don't fight as well as I'd like." I lost my usual saintly composure long enough to say, "Go cry on someone else's shoulder about how these enormous trout 'don't fight as well as you'd like.' I mean, what do you *want*?"

After a number of years—a number that varies from place to place depending on dozens of cryptic factors—the new reservoir begins to decline as the artificially large biomass settles into something a little more normal, something it can maintain. It can still be good, but not *as* good. Local anglers will blame this on everything from out-of-state fishermen to nuclear testing.

Other things can happen as well. At Spinney, suckers appeared and then pike. They weren't stocked, but according to the biologists, both were in the drainage, and infestations were inevitable.

We humans try desperately to think of things in static terms. Certain values are enduring, certain countries are friendly, certain lakes have big fish. It lets us relax a little, or it would if it were true. The fact is, a few isolated things do endure, but most of what we deal with is more accurately thought of as a process rather than a monument.

In the grand scheme, there can be moments in the lives of reservoirs that are glorious, but they seldom last forever. For instance, the trout fishery in Spinney is now beginning to fade, the pike fishery is on the upswing, and the sucker fishery would be fabulous if there was any earthly use for suckers.

The moment I think I can see coming is the one when a generation of trout, peaking on the increased food supply and beginning to grow old, will get as big as they can possibly be under the circumstances. At the same time, perhaps, the pike, new to the water, will quickly grow large and fat by eating up all the smaller trout and suckers. They'll be as big as they're going to get, too. Maybe they'll even boost the size of the big trout a little by thinning out the competition for the available food. Who knows?

Picture a cold early spring day, maybe this year, maybe next, when the huge cutthroats are stacked up outside the river inlets getting ready to spawn and when the monstrous, ugly, toothy pike are beginning to nose into the weedy shallows—also on that end of the lake, also to spawn.

Can you see it? The month is April, or maybe early May. Even the sun is cool, and storm after storm tears off the Continental Divide and slides across South Park. The sky and the water both go from chilly blue to light dun to slate. The lines of the round, modest hills are sparse and Oriental with little detail, making the eye sweep for miles at a glance.

You're one of the few hard-core types bobbing in float tubes or huddled in anchored, but still pitching, boats; bundled in elaborate layers of warm clothing, but still cold. You could even be alone out there, but that's not likely anymore. This foul-weather fishing business isn't the secret it was even a decade ago.

Fishing a weighted streamer (maybe the size 2 olive and black Weedless Wooley that has worked before) you hook one heavy fish after another. The fly is fished erratically, with fast pulls, pauses, twitches, because you sense the mood of the prespawning fish. It's one of the things we have in common with them: that not unwelcome panicky aggravation that comes from being glommed upon by an inexplicable horniness.

You handle and release them with numbing hands, and, because they're so much bigger than you're used to, you have no clear idea of what they weigh. You might put one on the scale to get a general picture of things, but then you'll start fighting the urge to kill one to mount and hang on the wall. This would cost hundreds of dollars and would freeze a beautiful and tragic instant in your fishing career that should probably be allowed to pass.

There's poetry to great fishing, but I would stuff a 10-pound cutthroat. I wouldn't be able to stop myself—and no one would blame me.

After writing those last few paragraphs I had to go out and sit on the front steps and pet the cat for a while to calm down. It's January 25th, a Sunday when most normal people are watching Denver play New York in the Super Bowl. I'm expected to follow football even though I don't, but I've developed a ploy to conceal my ambivalence. Someone will say, "How 'bout that game Sunday," and I'll answer, "Yeah, boy."

It's almost fifty degrees, partly sunny, a sweet breeze blowing: one of those cruel hints of spring we get here in Colorado at a time of year when most of our snow is yet to fall. Still, all this stuff I've been raving about could happen in eight weeks.

If it happens at all.

There's a rumor going around to the effect that it *will* happen, but I think I started it. Like most fishing rumors about upcoming events, it's wishful thinking with some loosely woven basis in fisheries biology; an obscure field, but not as obscure as life in general. In both cases, you make a guess and take your best shot, although in fishing you'll at least know when you were right.

In the end, it's inevitable. I'll have to go up there and suffer in the cold for a few days because sometimes what you think you see is actually there.

There are two schools of thought about fly-fishing prairie lakes. One school tries to imitate every possible food organism in these rich waters on the premise that the trout are gourmets; they see so many bugs and such that they can pick and choose, feeding selectively, capriciously changing their tastes from day to day, if not hour to hour.

Most of these folks are flytiers who have as much fun at the vise as they do on the water.

The other school is the one Wyoming Willie belongs to. These guys say the trout see so many different bugs that they *don't* become selective, but feed casually on this and that as they stumble into it. These fishermen tend to use a handful of general fly patterns. Willie favored the Hares Ear Nymph in size 8 and a green Damselfly Nymph, also large, in a lake where you'd have to tow a spare belly boat to carry copies of all the items on the menu.

So, two groups of serious fly-fishers have looked at the same set of facts and have come up with opposing theories. Imagine that. Even more interesting, both catch fish.

What seems to happen is this: When not much is happening and the fish are cruising around lazily, yes, they'll often move for the general pattern, possibly as much out of curiosity and the general principles of the predator as out of pressing hunger. Remember, these trout are in fish heaven with a largely unlimited food supply. Except at spawning times, they seldom hit hard or act greedy.

But then when there's a concentration of food forms, they can turn very picky, refusing flies that are a size too big or the wrong color and taking even the naturals with a studied lack of concern.

Usually. Often. Nine times out of ten, that is.

Those are the two extremes, but there are many gradations of behavior in between. These fish are moody and, like us, their moods don't come from nowhere. What they do reflects what they are and what's happening in their environment at the moment. This doesn't mean the answer is clear, but it means there *is* an answer, which is nice to know.

On that first day on the nameless lake in Wyoming, it was hit and miss (with a few hits) until late afternoon when the caddis hatch Willie had warned us about began to come off. He'd said the flies were big, but that left me unprepared. The prairie lakes can grow hefty caddis flies, but these were the size of grasshoppers, a good two hook sizes longer than the biggest caddis fly I had with me.

I've seen hatches of monster lake caddis before, and they've all done what these did. They hatched into the winged adults at the surface and then ran around on top of the water for a few minutes before taking off. They looked like biplanes taxiing around a field trying to get into the wind, except the wings of the bugs were folded.

In times past, mostly on cold mountain lakes, this kind of fishing was pleasantly easy. You tie on the biggest dry fly you have, lob it out there, and haul it around. Pretty soon a trout eats it. Alternatively, you can tie on one of your big nymphs, maybe a size 4, and do the same thing to imitate the emerging pupae. It's not uncommon for the fish to lose their usual trouty caution and chase the big bugs all over the lake. It's the kind of thing you love to see, especially on a difficult lake, because it means you're about to catch a bunch of fish.

Usually.

My biggest caddis patterns were of the Elk Hair variety and turned out to be too stubby in the body, too heavy in the wing, too fuzzy in the hackle, and too dark in color. At least that's how they looked to me, and I figured the trout were thinking pretty much the same thing when they'd swim over to look at one and then turn away in obvious disgust as if to say, "What does he think he's fishing for, bass?"

Scissored down some, they worked no better and looked considerably worse.

Then I tried a grasshopper pattern (I'd made that connection, hadn't I?). It looked pretty good to me, but not to the fish.

I'd landed two rainbows that day—one about 5 and one about 6 pounds—on a streamer and a nymph, but I wanted desperately to catch one of those hogs on a dry fly.

It was getting dark. Willie hooked one on a Hares Ear Nymph.

I was getting nervous. I knew the hatch would come off the following evening, and I could picture exactly how I'd copy the bug in fur and feathers if I'd had my travel fly tying kit along, but I *didn't* have it. I'd foolishly left it at home thinking, too short a trip, limited room in the car, etc. Dumb.

Of course, I have the flies now. They're sparsely tied with a wheat-colored body, quill wing, sparse ginger hackle, and stripped ginger quill antennae on long-shanked, light wire #6 and #8 hooks. They're good-looking flies (if I do say so myself) although they may be a bit on the small side. I keep them in a plastic fly line box because they won't fit in the compartments of any of my normal fly boxes. I tied them the night after we got back, and I'm sure they're exactly right, no question about it. There are never any questions about these things once you're back home.

In a fit of magnanimity, I tied some extras and sent them to Willie, hoping for a small victory by association, but I learned a few weeks later by return mail that he had sold his motel in Warland and had moved to Big Sky, Montana.

Montana Willie? Nope, doesn't quite get it.

He wrote back to thank me. "They're really nice flies and will probably come in handy," he said.

I did manage a pair of hogs on dry flies, though. One was on a #14 Elk Hair Caddis that didn't copy anything on the water. He weighed somewhere around 5 pounds. The other was a 6-and-a-fraction-pound rainbow on a #16 dry midge: biggest trout of that season, the biggest ever on a dry fly and completely satisfactory.

Still, there's the gnawing reality that I didn't crack that hatch. The trout that took the dry caddis fly was the one Al McClane once wrote about: the fish that wants to be caught.

Maybe that's why fishing is such an appropriate allegory. Absolute perfection doesn't really exist, or if it does, you're left trying frantically to remember it; to freeze the fish in mid-jump like the painters do, although for some odd reason there's a kind of comfort in the futility of it all.

Then again, if I'd caught a damned fish on a big caddis fly, I probably wouldn't be talking like this.

At this writing, I haven't been back, but I just had lunch with

Jay during which the plan took shape. We'll fly to Bozeman where we'll meet Willie, pile into his car, and head for The Lake. Three or four days should give us a good, healthy shot at it. Jay had already talked with Willie, who is up for the trip. In fact, it was his idea. Jay quoted him as saying, "This time we'll get into the big ones," which leaves me wondering what we were catching the last time. Surely not the little ones.

We'll carry deflated belly boats, waders, flippers, a bundle of fly rods each, and duffels containing reels, lines, long johns, rain gear, and everything else we might need. It will be more than one man can carry for more than fifty yards at a stretch. I sometimes tell people I fly-fish in order to attain a kind of simplicity, but then when I go on the road I feel like a traveling theater troupe.

Unfortunately, my airplane program does not allow for the fly tying kit, which is bigger and heavier than most suitcases and is designed to be operated off the tailgate of a pickup truck. That bothers me a little, but you have to either draw the line somewhere or charter the whole plane.

On the other hand, I already have the flies—the ones Willie said were real nice—and I'm sure they'll work.

Absolutely sure.

No question about it.

When I was a young feller, I thought my Uncle Leonard had invented the concept of the fishing car; the elderly but still serviceable vehicle that was reserved for angling and angling-related activities to the extent that it was kept loaded, like the shotgun behind the kitchen door. But then I thought Leonard had invented a lot of things, some of which have since turned out to be among the oldest jokes in the world. It's understandable, I guess. In matters pertaining to fishing—not to mention farming, guitar playing, and a number of other things—he had the authority that comes from experience; and I was also into a bit of adolescent hero worship.

The idea of the fishing car spoke to me of a way of life. It was the thought that you could be a sportsman in the same way you could be a Baptist or a farmer or a blond; that being a fisherman could be as much a part of your identity as your fingerprints. And I was at the age where I had just started to puzzle over my identity.

The fishing car in those days was the "ambler." It had actually once said "Rambler" in chrome letters on the hood, but a minor run-in with a fence post had resulted in the abbreviated version. Of course, there was no thought of having it fixed.

It was a black station wagon with many thousands of miles on it that somehow always ran—after a little prodding—and that was always stocked with axes, minnow buckets, tackle boxes, rods, etc. The upholstery was ragged, the windshield was pitted, the dashboard was dusty, the tires were fair, and it had an aroma about it of beer, Coke, cleaned fish, wet wool, and a few other things that were hard to place. The exact opposite of that new car smell.

I don't know what ever happened to it, but, by all rights, it should have been bronzed and placed on a pedestal on the banks of a good bass pond somewhere in Indiana.

I spent as much time as I could with Leonard while I was growing up, and much of it passed in the front seat of the ambler following lazy, circuitous routes to one bass pond or another. We drove the dirt roads most of the time. Some were so little used that by midsummer the tall grass growing between the wheel ruts would slap the front bumper. The roads in those rural counties were laid out more or less on grids, and we got to where we were going by starting at a known point and then angling in what seemed like the right direction.

In the course of things we discovered several little towns that were doubtless unknown to the outside world; towns so slowly paced that a dog could safely sleep on the warm pavement of Main Street in the late afternoon, because everyone knew that Butch might be taking a nap in the road in front of the hardware store. Butch himself, a fair-to-middling hunting dog in his younger years, could live to the ripe age of eighteen or twenty, and when he finally passed away—quietly, in his sleep—the whole town would feel bad about it for a day or two.

Sometimes we'd stop and ask directions, which could be a laborious process. Everyone knew where everything was, but what was County Road 23 to us was usually the Road Out to the Jones Place to everyone else. I never saw Leonard use a store-bought map, but we followed several that were scratched on paper napkins or matchbook covers.

Leonard was a master at navigating in farm country, but we did occasionally get lost. This was known as "taking the scenic route." There were rare times when we never quite got to where we were going, but we always got *somewhere*.

Leonard made a point of appearing confident and in charge, so it was difficult to tell when he knew where he was and when he didn't. There were times when I'd have sworn we were hopelessly lost, but then we'd pull up to an unlocked gate that looked exactly like the last twenty unlocked gates we'd passed, and he would describe the pond that was still out of sight down a two-wheel dirt track: its size, its shape, the muddy bank, the cattails along the east side, everything. Of course, he did have the reputation of knowing where every bass and most of the panfish in three counties lived.

He also knew half the people in the same area, and if he *didn't* know them, he soon would. He was deeply in touch with the interlocking networks of relations, work, church, and grange that tied the farming community together, and all he needed to make a connection was a name off a mailbox.

It was something to see. Leonard would bounce the ambler up a perfectly strange driveway, negotiate through the dogs, find the owner (who was invariably poking at some broken piece of machinery), and deftly establish himself as a neighbor, if not an out-and-out friend of the family. There would then follow an interminable period of fence leaning, gravel kicking, sky squinting, and a rambling philosophical discussion that included everything from the hound dog at your feet to the President of the United States. Of the two, the dog was the more competent.

It took time, but sooner or later we'd end up catching large bass from an obscure pond that hadn't been fished five times in as many years. The farmer always got some cleaned fish out of it, and then we'd pile into the ambler and drive off, waving at a man who was now our friend or who, at the very least, was too polite to say no to a couple of nice enough guys.

Driving home at night it would occur to me that, although life would surely provide some interruptions, there'd be nothing wrong with doing this all the time.

Of all the trips Leonard and I took in that car, the one I remember most clearly was our longest and last. My family had moved to Minnesota, and I hadn't seen Leonard in a while. I was a teenager then, having attained some height and a considerable dose of that quality that was once known as strong-headedness. My mother smiles about those years now, but Dad didn't live quite long enough to see all the humor in it. Maybe strong-headed is too mild a term.

Dad and I did hunt and fish together, though, and that was our one stable point of agreement through some years that could easily have ended in a complete severing of diplomatic relations.

It was Dad who gave me my first view of fly-fishing. I'd read about it in the outdoor magazines and had even once seen a man using what was known back then in the Midwest as a "trout rod." Dad said he didn't know much about it, but that the people who practiced it were the true artists of the sport. Leonard gave me my second view. "Fly-fishermen are a bunch of conceited pricks," he said.

It took me a number of years to realize that both men were right.

You see, Dad was what you'd have to call a gentleman sportsman type. He would never have considered poaching or doing anything out of season; he loved fine tackle and thought it was vastly superior to catch a fish on a lure rather than bait, because this actually involved fooling the game with your skill and cunning. Leonard, on the other hand, fished to catch fish, which he then killed and ate. He respected private property, but he also believed that God had put fish on the earth for all the people, and these two ideas constantly battled for his soul. His gear was wired, glued, and duct-taped together, and he fished with whatever it took, stopping short only of explosives, and then only because they'd have been too loud.

If I'd actually set out to get a perfectly balanced education as a fisherman, I couldn't have chosen two better teachers.

Where was I? Right. The longest and last trip in the ambler.

It so happened that my sister decided to get married one summer not long after we'd moved to Minnesota, a state that was full of lakes which were, in turn, lousy with fish. Weeks before the actual festivities, the family began to gather. By the time Leonard and Aunt Dora arrived, the house was filled with grannies and aunts and mobs of cousins on the way.

Leonard and I got together out in the backyard, where it was quiet, and decided the best thing for us to do was go wet a line somewhere, just to get out from underfoot, you understand. We packed quickly, left quietly, and drove north in the ambler.

We drove for some eighteen or twenty hours, watching the landscape go from fields to scattered groves to coniferous forests and feeling the hot closeness of the summer air become cool and sharply scented with pine. Somewhere along the line we turned off the main highway onto a dirt county road.

Up there the roads were fewer and farther between than in rural Indiana and anything but straight. They didn't seem to go much of anywhere, but all roads go somewhere, and we finally pulled up to a medium-sized lake with tree-lined banks and water lilies as if it had been our destination from the start. We rented a small, rickety cabin that came with an equally small and rickety rowboat. Both leaked, but were thoughtfully equipped with the appropriate tin cans.

In the days that followed, we caught fish.

There were foot-long perch in the little bay right outside the cabin door that came into the boat with the kind of regularity you somehow only remember from long ago. On the first night we sat down to baked beans from a can and a platter of breaded and fried perch fillets from a lake that neither of us had seen or even heard of before. Definitely the way to begin a fishing trip.

We took smallmouth bass from around the rocky points on small floating lures and spoons. They were an olivish-bronze color and jumped the way I would later learn that rainbow trout do.

The northern pike came from deeper water to big, heavy Johnson's Weedless Spoons trailing strips of pickled pork rind. They were my favorites, being large, prehistorically ugly, and—by stretching the imagination some—even a little dangerous. Leonard said the real fight with a big pike began when you got him in the boat. In any case, there were some minor injuries, complete with blood, and I loved it.

During the middle of some days, we drove around the back roads to look at other lakes and talk to sellers of bait and renters of boats, all of whom were getting their share of fish that week. "Getting our share" is one of those wonderful fishing euphemisms that sound promising, but that can mean damn near anything.

As I said, Leonard was a great raconteur of the fence-leaning or one-foot-up-on-the-dock-piling school, and he enjoyed talking and joking with fishermen as much as he liked fishing itself. He was good at it, too. He knew that few fishermen, himself included, would tell a stranger what he needed to know straight out, so he assembled information not so much by the facts as by evaluating the empty space around them. He taught me, for example, not to pay attention to the lures that were well stocked, regardless of how pretty they were or how hard the sales pitch was, but to always ask what had once hung on the empty pegs. The ones that were sold out were the ones that caught fish.

I guess it took me a long time to come to appreciate the charms and real advantages of just *talking* about fishing, looking at water, leaning on things, reading between lines. At the time I was a little impatient. You remember, it was childhood; the days of wooden rowboats when men who didn't know each other could stand and chew the fat for hours. But I knew I'd be doing it myself someday, so I paid attention and mostly kept my mouth shut in the borrowed style of the strong, silent type. The compliment I was being paid was that of being left to myself—of not having to be watched and kept amused. Back home I felt like a man who was being treated like a boy. Out fishing with Leonard, it was the other way around.

Then, as now, these conversations tended to dissolve around late afternoon when the first boils could be seen out along the weed beds. There was a slow, satisfying logic about it all.

I drove the ambler on many of those back roads, not because I was allowed to, as I'd been in the past, but because a fishing partner shares the driving chores. Never mind that I was too young to have a license.

It wasn't until a few hours before the wedding—not quite the last possible moment—that we strolled in the back door sublimely unconcerned, wearing clothes we'd fished in for a week and carrying armloads of fillets. The house was in a uniform state of hysteria: the women were all at a dead run or off in a corner weeping, while the men were looking mounted in suits that had last been worn at funerals. I've since come to recognize the pained, furtive look they wore as symptomatic of the powerful need for a drink.

"It's about time," someone said, and we were grabbed by the ears and forcibly washed. The story is told that our clothes had to be burned, but that may be an exaggeration. I've never felt less welcome arriving at an event I was supposed to attend.

I remember coming downstairs to the kitchen all clean and dressed up and running into Dad. He'd been stuffed into a tuxedo and was fondling a big glass of bourbon with a single, lonely ice cube floating in it. We were alone, but the sound of chattering washed in from the front room.

"Caught some fish," Dad said (not a question).

"Yup," I answered, all puffed up with teenage conceit and vanity.

He raised his glass slightly in a toast and flashed me an evil little grin, something between envy, pride, and resignation. Now that I think about it, maybe he *did* see the humor in it now and then, or if not the humor, then something. Dad always tried to be strict and straight-laced with me, but word around the family was he'd had his moments as a young man. I remember wanting to tell him I'd driven the car for hundreds of miles, and then thinking I'd best not push my luck.

I've traveled in a number of fishing cars since then, from a Volkswagen that must have been a contemporary of the ambler to a gas-guzzling road slug that blotted out the sun as it passed by. Each has had a certain romance about it, based not so much on its looks or performance as on what it was, where it had been, and where it might be going next.

Koke has a station wagon now that will be just fine after a little breaking in, but he used to own one of the most famous fishing cars in the Rocky Mountain West. I remember it as a Ford, while A.K. swears it was a Dodge. Odd. Whatever make it was, it was big and white with a combination boat-and-rod rack on the roof and the biggest trunk I've ever seen.

Somewhere in this trunk you could find anything any three people would need on a month-long fishing trip, except that you couldn't find anything if you weren't Koke. The stuff was there in layers, like at an archeological dig, and if you were asked to get something ("It's right on top, you can't miss it."), it could take an hour, during which time you'd come across a dozen articles of tackle that had gone out of production twenty years ago. It became a simile, as in, "What have you been doing? This place looks like Koke's trunk."

A.K. himself has a good one now, a vintage Chevrolet pickup with a 400-some cubic inch V-8 and a camper shell. One of the first custom features he installed was an electric lantern hung just inside the back hatch for de-rigging in the dark, something we end up doing on three out of four trips.

On one of our recent expeditions, A.K.'s tent blew down in a wind that was not quite bad enough to make us get our belly boats off the water (which, I think, speaks volumes of ill about the tent), and we ended up sleeping in the truck. It was a pain at the time because all the float tubes, spare waders, fly tying travel kits, spare rods, camp kitchen, and such had to be unloaded in the dark and stowed under tarps, because it was raining as well as blowing. But in the end I think it was fitting. A car that hasn't been slept in on an emergency basis isn't quite broken in.

Then there's my own succession of fishing cars. There was a white International Scout and then a blue and white Scout that had once been a U.S. Mail truck and had the steering wheel on the wrong side. It was a conversation piece, but that's about the best I can say for it. Both cars were tinny, didn't have enough room in the back, and the four-cylinder engines were too weak. Great for delivering mail, but not too hot for fishing.

Why two of them? I'd just given up on the first one as being not enough truck when a guy who owed me $400—and who was not about to get the cash and who was also about to leave town suddenly for some reason—gave me the second one to clear the debt. "Thanks a lot," I said.

People assumed that I loved Scouts because I had a pair of them.

Those were followed by the longest running fishing car to date, a 1966 red Ford three-quarter-ton pickup with a long bed, a big engine, and four-wheel drive. It was a ten-mile-to-the-gallon monster that was, if anything, too much truck rather than too little. Still, I had great luck with it, partly because it was a solid vehicle with lots of spirit and partly because I had aged some by then, learning some lessons in the process. One lesson was that four-wheel drive doesn't mean you can go anywhere, it just means you can get stuck in worse places.

In his formative months, my late bird dog (and I use the term lightly) was left in the cab and, with nothing better to do, ate the seat on the driver's side. "Why didn't you chew up *your* side?" I asked, but he just wagged his tail and smiled, happy to see me. That dog lived for almost sixteen years, but he never got any more considerate.

Once, while hauling a load of firewood out of the National Forest on a muddy road, I skidded sideways against a ponderosa pine tree and bashed in the left door, closing and locking it permanently, but otherwise doing little damage. I didn't really mind having to get in on the wrong side and slide across, although I did tear the back pockets off more than one pair of jeans on the exposed springs. And it wasn't all that pretty when I got it, either, having once been a yard truck at a lumber mill.

You get the picture.

I got so attached to that truck that I honestly cried when it went the way of all flesh, having de-evolved from a powerful, soulful V-8 into a pitiful, wheezing V-6½. I kept the gearshift knob as a souvenir, because even that had a heavy, well-built feel to it. I haven't seen it in a while, though. One of my ex-cats used to like to play with it, so it's probably under the couch now. The cat, Maggie, also had soul. She died a few years ago in a valiant, if misguided, attempt to eat a rattlesnake. The cat got a decent burial, but I don't own enough land, nor the right equipment, to inter a pickup truck.

You may have noticed I have a thing for big American trucks. Some of that is pure genetic patriotism, but there are also some practical considerations.

I buy inexpensive vehicles, for reasons that will become obvious if you ever drop by the place here, and big old American trucks are cheap. They're also well built, heavy, and they're powerful if the rings are still okay. They do burn a lot of gas, but you have to look at that closely. You can buy a $12,000 pickup that gets twenty-three miles to the gallon of no-lead, or you can buy a $1,000 gunboat that gets eight miles to a gallon of regular. Work it out yourself. How many miles do you have to drive to save $11,000 in gas money?

Your big old pickup will also carry a lot of gear and will sleep two comfortably under the basic camper shell. If you ever break down (it's a fair bet you will), you'll open the hood of your venerable machine to find an engine block, valve covers, starter motor, fuel pump, distributor, carburetor . . . you know, the usual parts. If you're a fair-to-middling roadside mechanic with a wrench, screwdriver, a pair of pliers, and maybe a hammer, it will all make a certain sense. The motors in new trucks look like time machines and, anyway, the problem could be a computer malfunction.

If your old truck looks seedy enough, it's also the last one in the parking lot anyone would think of breaking into, which can be a real advantage. On a normal outing, the gear in my truck is worth more than the vehicle itself.

Along those same lines, I was once told by a retired police officer to remove the decals on my back window, you know, the ones that tell the world what organizations I belong to. "All they do is tell the bad guys what kind of merchandise is probably inside," he said.

Something to think about.

The worst is the one that says, "This Vehicle Insured by Smith & Wesson." It doesn't scare anyone, but it tells them there's probably a valuable handgun under the seat.

You get attached to an old heap, but you don't worry about it like you would a shiny new one. I once left the Ford in a bus stop parking lot for three days while I was off fishing the Frying

Pan and Roaring Fork rivers with Koke. When I got back the truck was as I'd left it, except that most of the gas had been siphoned from the tank and the gas cap was missing. On the plus side, it hadn't been broken into or vandalized. I can almost picture the bum standing there thinking, "Well, there's probably nothing in it, and as for smashing it up for kicks, it looks like someone has beat me to it."

I had enough fuel left to get to a town and buy some more, and, since I'd been happily catching trout for three days (during which time I never once stopped to worry about the truck), I decided to feel charitable. It is, after all, easy enough to construct a scenario where some destitute fellow human being is trying to get from point A to point B without enough money for gas, possibly on a very important errand. A job, maybe, or a death in the family or a girlfriend. Something crucial.

And the gas cap? Well, maybe he just dropped it. It was dark and I was tired. I didn't even look.

As an interim measure, I stuck one of those red mechanics' rags where the cap should have gone. It worked fine, and I didn't get a real store-bought gas cap until someone asked me if I'd decided to turn the truck into a Molotov cocktail and go on a suicide mission.

There's just something *about* the older American pickups. They're like model 94 Winchester rifles or Granger fly rods: ordinary and workmanlike, but still classy and dripping with romance. To drive one is to make a statement about enduring values. It's a way of identifying yourself, in this big, sprawling culture of ours, as a guy who occasionally has to haul stuff.

Of course, it's a personal matter, and there is another side to all this. Last winter I jokingly said to a friend of mine—the owner of a new Oriental recreational vehicle—that a real man drives an American pickup. In an impressively level way, he replied that a real man drives whatever he, by God, pleases.

Okay.

The old blue Chevy pickup I have now—referred to in some circles as The Blue Streak and in others as Old Blue—is a serviceable truck, though it has not quite become the cosmic fishing car. These things take time, not to mention the proper accumulation of adventures and mishaps.

It has some streamer flies and a bass bug stuck in the dashboard, which is a nice, homey touch, and is chugging away on its second used engine. It took me through Wyoming, Idaho, and Montana last summer with only one small electrical problem that was easily fixed, though not so easily diagnosed. It's never let me down seriously except for the time it caught fire at the corner of Canyon Boulevard and 28th Street in Boulder, Colorado. During rush hour. I had no idea so many people carried fire extinguishers in their cars.

Still, it's seventeen years old, and to fix everything that is wrong, or about to *go* wrong, would cost too much. So it's on its way out. I'll always fondly remember tying flies on its tailgate, but I can't trust it far from home anymore.

Buying a new (old) pickup is like fishing a new pond that you know nothing about. It could be full of big fish; it could also be full of alkali—not only fishless, but poisoned. Over the years I have learned the following things:

It will be hard to find, but you want one with a bunged up body that's still in working order. Most people are embarrassingly superficial in this regard and will pay more for a smooth body and a good paint job than for a truck that actually runs. Don't even look under the hood, just take it somewhere and have the compression checked. Then tell the guy who's selling it that it looks like hell.

The shape the bed is in will tell you more about a pickup than any other single thing. If the bed is all dented and scratched up, it was a work truck and was probably used hard. Is the tailgate bunged up on the top edge? It means a lot of heavy stuff was loaded and unloaded. Is the tailgate *missing?* Bad sign. So much stuff was loaded that it got in the way and they took it off.

Well, not always. A missing tailgate combined with a clean, almost pristine bed probably means that a camper sat there until very recently.

What you want is a ten- or twelve-year-old pickup that was used recreationally a few times a year by a seventy-five-year-old fisherman who doesn't kick ass like he used to and who does his running around town in his wife's sedan.

With even some of the used trucks now being too tinny and having too many moving parts to be reasonable, I'm beginning to think the answer is to get hold of a good, solid, well-seasoned pickup and commit to whatever it takes to keep it running for the rest of my life. This would solve a number of problems and would also be a big step toward firmly establishing me as an old fart, something I believe to be the secret, lifelong ambition of every serious fisherman.

I'm fully aware that somewhere down the road I'll run head-on into the fact that nothing can or does last forever. That's one of the reasons why I've never tried to find that lake and that cabin up in Minnesota again. You and I both know what has surely happened there by now. It would be like coming on the ambler rotting away in a field somewhere with the windows shot out.

I guess my sister got married okay that summer, although I can't say I actually remember the ceremony. All the fish got eaten, and Leonard and I were eventually forgiven, though I've never been quite sure what for.

When it was all over, I walked Leonard and Aunt Dora out to the fishing car. They were headed back to Indiana, and the ambler didn't look right with suitcases and garment bags in it. Leonard and I ran down some brief, vague plans for future fishing trips, and then, with nothing left to say, they drove off. As it turned out, I would never see the ambler again, and Leonard and I would never fish together again, either, although I didn't know that at the time. You never know those things at the time.

The last time I saw it, the car was still dusty from the trip to the lake. Aunt Dora had wanted to have it washed, but there just wasn't time.

THE
PURIST

What is it about fly-fishing that attracts purists, those people who must engineer a corner of their lives— sometimes a pretty large corner— where things have to be done properly? I'm not sure I know, but whatever it is, it's why the sport can be used to define the very existence of the practitioner. If you're into it long enough, sooner or later someone will say, "He's one of those misanthropic fly-fishing types," and everyone will know what they mean.

I'm not one of those guys who grew up with a fly rod. Instead, I grew up with a bait-casting rod, tackle box, and, yes, a can of worms. It was okay. In fact, it was a hell of a lot of fun, and it worked just fine for me until I came face to face with fly-fishing. That didn't happen until I was in my early twenties.

When my college graduation rolled around, I was working as a plumber's helper in, of all places, Cleveland, Ohio, getting some money up to get the car fixed and head west. I had somehow managed to finish four years at college and still be three credits short of a degree, so I was working days and writing nights on an independent study paper.

It was awful; not the writing or the work, but Cleveland. The only favorable thing I can say about it is that back then you could hear some good music if you wanted to take your life in your hands to go to the clubs. At twenty-one you're more than willing to do that, because it's clear you're immortal.

They say Lake Erie is coming back now and you can even eat the fish you catch from it without fear of brain damage, but in those days it was a fetid, stinking thing that would give you a rash if you even got close to it. In fact, it was along in there somewhere that the Cuyahoga River (a "river" in name only) caught fire and burned for days. I don't know how I ended up there, but I knew I had to get out, and fast, good rhythm and blues or not.

The plumber I was helping was a man named John Gray, and when I announced at the end of one work day that I would be quitting in a week to attend graduation, get my sheepskin, and then leave the state at the greatest possible speed, he asked, "What's your degree in?"

"Philosophy," I answered.

"Well," he said, "I guess you'll be leavin' the plumbing business and hanging your shingle out somewhere."

I never knew if he was kidding or not, but on the long drive across Kansas I considered it. I could hang my diploma on the wall and put a sign out front saying:

PHILOSOPHER

Reasonable rates—no waiting
No question too large
No question too small

I had no idea what to do with my life and it seemed as good as anything. It was also the only thing I was trained for—I hadn't even learned plumbing.

Instead, I ended up working various labor jobs and found that the western U.S. was lousy with bearded young men with college degrees who had also turned their backs on the establishment and were more or less happily driving nails and digging ditches. In the 1960s, many of the crews were made up of quasi-intellectual types, and sometimes we'd spend a few hours at Tom's Tavern after work discussing whether essence precedes existence or vice versa over some cold ones.

In Boulder, Colorado, where I settled after some months of wandering around, there was even a joke about it:

A guy applies for a carpentry job, and when the foreman asks about his education, he says, "I have a master's degree in English literature."

"Sorry, kid," the foreman says. "We're looking for someone with a Ph.D."

I was in sparse touch with my folks then—without much in the way of a permanent address or phone number—and when we did talk they tended to wonder what I'd be doing about a career. No problem. By then it had become clear: I was going to be a writer (a *serious* writer) and an equally serious fly-fisherman, not necessarily in that order. In the meantime, I would work labor by day, play blues guitar by night, think deep thoughts, and, as it turned out, get married and divorced so quickly it would have made my head spin if it hadn't been spinning already. As so often happens, the final dispute wasn't over politics, philosophy, or even faithfulness; it was over brown rice. Macrobiotic or not, I was sick of it.

I saw the whole thing as a revealing detail, an insight, fodder for the great surrealist novel I'd be getting to work on any day now.

Fly-fishing was, of course, perfect. It was solitary, meditative (if not brooding), enigmatic, and properly Bohemian. Going by the stereotype, at least, it was practiced by tweedy, thoughtful types who exuded a low-key but constant literary hum, if for no other reason than that so many good books had been written about the sport.

It was also quite beautiful.

But the best thing was, it led you inexorably to one paradox after another. The idea was to catch fish, but the best writers made it evident that it was perfectly okay not to as long as you failed to catch them with the proper grace and style.

The catch-and-release ethic was just beginning to blossom then, so if you actually did catch a trout, you'd probably release it. The fisheries management logic behind this was flawless, and that's why fly-fishers practiced it—but it's not why they *liked* it.

They liked it for its Zen flavor. Yin and yang—fish and no fish—it's all the same. "Trout" is defined only by the absence of trout surrounding it. Good day or bad, the creel remains empty, except maybe for a couple of beers. It was a kind of poetic game that you could win simply by coming to understand the rules.

I thought of it as a case of personal enlightenment at the time—as you think of everything in the first few years of legal drinking age—but it turned out that thousands of my fellow hippie baby boomers had seen the same light. I'd only been at it for a few years when the late Arnold Gingrich—one of the great old fly-fishing gentlemen—said he no longer had to apologize for the sport; that fully half of the best fly-fishers he knew were under thirty.

The rules.

They came from England, not from Izaak Walton, who was, in fact, a bank-napping bait fisherman, but from Halford and that bunch of chalk-stream types. To them a fly was a dry fly; not only that, it was a *may*fly; not only that, it was cast upstream to rising trout. End of discussion. Anything else is poaching.

There didn't seem to be any reasoning behind this, but remember, it happened in England.

Also in that country, G.E.M. Skues legitimized the wet fly by tying it to imitate a mayfly nymph and calling it that: a nymph.

After trashing our brook trout fisheries along the East Coast, we Americans imported the brown trout from Europe along with the British ethics and techniques that had grown up around that fish.

We also imported English-style naturalism, and the Catskill flytiers began to fashion trout flies on English models that looked like our bugs. They worked, and we still fish many of them.

Somewhere along the line, the naturalists hooked up with the entomologists, and Ernest Schwiebert eventually wrote *Matching the Hatch*. It wasn't the first book on angling entomology, or the last, but it was the one that made its title part of the language. Today you can find fly-fishers who talk about how they've been matching the hatch, but who have never even read the book.

By this time it was permissible, among the intelligentsia at least, to fish with flies imitating any insect, crustacean, bait fish, or whatever that a trout might eat—on or below the surface—with the possible exception of the salmon egg. In fact, studies were quoted to the effect that trout did 80 percent (or some other large percentage, depending on which expert you read) of their feeding under the surface, and the implication was that the smart fisherman—the *effective* fisherman—would fish with nymphs most of the time.

Of course, "nymph" was no longer the broad term that wet fly had once been. Suddenly there were nymphs, larvae, and pupae, depending on the species of bug in question.

Fly-fishing had begun to become scientific, or at least the terminology of science began to sneak into the sport. Most who go after it seriously now know the life cycles of the major trout stream insects and can tell the difference between the various bugs in their various stages. To many the Green Drake is now an Ephemerella grandis, and the Blue-winged Olive is really a Baetis, although I'm told by those who know that the Green Drake could actually be the glacialis, doddsi, hecuba, or the coloradensis. On the other hand, the *Little* Green Drake is almost surely the Ephemerella flavalinea. If you're cool, you'll refer to it as a Flav. Latin slang.

Oddly enough, the scientific Latin is commonly used only on the mayflies. The same fisherman who tells you about the Ephemerella hatch in the afternoon will refer to the caddis that emerge that same evening as big gray ones or little olive ones. Larry Solomon and Eric Leiser made a valiant attempt to change that some years ago with their fine book *The Caddis and the Angler*, but, at least on the waters I fish, caddis flies continue to be described in terms of size and color alone. The few who insist on talking about the Brachycentrus hatch (#16 brown) have to translate for the rest of us. And yes, we're impressed.

The first people I fished with were cowboys. Well, they didn't actually ride horses and punch cows, but they did chew Red Man and they did wear those big hats. Remember, I was still new to the West. They fished with fly rods in small, secluded mountain streams and beaver ponds, and that's what I wanted: breathtaking scenery and trout.

I got both, but I caught my first trout on bait—worms and, in season, grasshoppers. The time came when I was ashamed of that and even lied about it, or at least carefully failed to mention it. Now it doesn't haunt me, I just don't do it anymore. And, actually, a long fly rod is probably the ideal tool for taking trout on bait from small streams. It's a time-honored method among old-timers around here.

My friends in the Stetson hats did occasionally fish flies. They'd carry a ratty handful in something like a Prince Albert tobacco can, things like Black Gnats, Gray Hackle Yellows, Royal Coachmen, and they'd fish them on the surface, "just like you would a live hopper."

Not unimportantly, I managed to lose my virginity by actually catching, handling, admiring, and even eating a few small brook trout.

"So this is trout fishing."

"Yeah, but it's not *fly*-fishing." Even the cowpokes admitted that.

It's not difficult to learn how to fly-fish, by which I mean it *is* difficult, but there are people who can teach you, and there are books, and volumes of magazine articles, and even video tapes. It's now possible to become an expert without ever catching a fish, or at least to sound like an expert.

What's really hard, though, is to get a handle on what the sport is actually about. You arrive at a view by osmosis—by being around fly-fishing and the people who do it—because the values are implied or assumed but seldom flatly stated. There does seem to be a kind of built-in moral tone to it, but mostly we tend to just figure it out as we go along.

There are those who live by the code: "Fly-fishing only." These are the purists who prefer the fly rod because it's poetic, graceful, and old, and also because it's hard to master. In fact, it's *impossible* to master. However good you get, there will always be casts you can't make and fish you can't catch.

The purist fishes exclusively with a fly rod, which means that he owns a spinning rod and sometimes uses it, but he doesn't take it seriously, doesn't talk about it much (is, to tell the truth, a little embarrassed about it), and stores it separately from his fly tackle.

Chances are it's a very good rod.

The snob is exactly like the purist except he doesn't own a spinning rod. He used to, but he gave it away years ago, not wanting to have the filthy thing around the house. Furthermore, anyone who does fish with a spinning rod is sleazy and cheap and his parents probably weren't married. This guy is not nice, or very happy either, and the time will surely come when he gets pretty lonely, too. Snobbery occurs as the result of a logical fallacy. We all want to experience and appreciate something of excellent quality, but it doesn't follow that we're every bit as good as what we do.

Granted, fly-fishing breeds its share of snobs, but so do other disciplines. There were, for instance, a number of them involved in the Spanish Inquisition.

You'd have to say the ultimate purist is the one who fishes only dry flies, with no exceptions. If the fish can't be caught on dries, they can't be caught. I know some people who have flirted with that approach, but none have stayed righteous. All that frenzied activity beneath the surface film was just too tantilizing. I have, however, heard stories and firmly believe such fishermen exist—probably back East somewhere.

I do know lots of people who *prefer* the dry fly, although they'll fish beneath the surface if they have to. A.K. and I are both like that, which is one of several reasons why we get along so well and have fished happily together for so long. We both believe that a 12-inch trout caught on a dry fly is four inches longer than a 12-inch trout caught on a nymph or streamer. It's something many fly-fishermen believe, or feel in their hearts. "And we got 'em on dry flies," they say, as if it couldn't have been any better. Maybe it's a lingering taste of that stern old English tradition. The sport does still have a faint eccentric British aroma to it, although I think I've smelled it less and less in recent years.

Wherever the idea comes from, the dry fly still exerts a kind of tyranny. You can take rising fish fairly on other kinds of flies, but you can't take them *properly* on anything but a dry.

Once A.K. and I were fishing twenty yards apart, in a line with several other fly-fishers who were also evenly spaced, to a fine Pale Morning Dun hatch, and nothing was working. I tried various dry flies (of course), various emergers, and a couple of floating nymphs.

Nothing.

I don't know what everyone else was trying, but every time I glanced up or downstream, one out of three anglers was rooting around in his fly box. Not a fish had been hooked in nearly an hour.

As the hatch began to peter off and doom was approaching, I tied on a #4 bucktail streamer—a trick, if you want to call it that, that had worked for me before. I slapped it against the bank, twitched it out twice, and had a sweet 16-inch rainbow.

It's what you dream of: not only hooking a nice fish with a large enough audience, but hooking the *only* fish. My shoulders squared. My head swelled. Everyone looked. I knew A.K. was going to deflate me (he considers it his job); I just didn't know how.

He called upstream: "What'd ya get him on?"

"Streamer," I said.

"Shit. If I'd known you was gonna fish bait I wouldn't have brought ya."

I guess the point is, no one really felt that way, but everyone laughed.

The idea of remaining somehow pure—in a largely undefined way—seems to permeate the sport of fly-fishing. The worst you can say about a questionable angling method is, "It's just like bait-fishing," or "Hell, you can do that on a spinning rod."

A.K. and I belong to the fairly small, but still vital, fly-fishing subculture that has settled on split cane rods as unquestionably top drawer, although we are not what you call steadfast about that. We both own some graphite rods and even fish them now and then, usually in situations that demand some kind of thunderstick, like a 10-foot, 8-weight. We have agreed that it's best not to try to defend cane in the company of graphite and neo–space age boron aficionados. Cane rods are just strange (these days) and old. Even the new ones, of which there are plenty, are "old" in a pleasantly kinky way.

It recently occurred to me that I got into cane rods, some years ago now, because almost everyone was impressed by them and, by implication, impressed by their users as well. I've stayed with them partly from habit, partly because I like them, and in *large* part because it now freaks so many people out.

This is what the purist does, be he fly-fisherman, collector of old cars, or whatever: he settles on a time in the past when it (whatever "it" is) was as good as it ever got. He also understands the considerable implications of that. When he says, "They don't make 'em like they used to," he means, "and they could if they wanted to, but they don't, and I don't understand why."

Some fly-fishers try to go back as far as possible in search of some kind of enlightenment. Among them are the people who are buying the pre–split cane style solid greenheart rods now being offered by the Partridge company.

To be completely unspoiled, one might actually have to regress back to silk lines and gut leaders. Silkworm gut is hard to come by now, but I did once try a silk line out of curiosity. It was a 33-yard Hedge "Balanced, anti-fly splash" (whatever that means) line that cast beautifully, but had to be unspooled, dried, and re-dressed every half-hour. It was authentic as hell, but also a pain. When, during a drying session one August, a bunch of grasshoppers chewed it to pieces while I took a nap, I wasn't all that disappointed.

Purity by nostalgia is an interesting idea, but the logic of it is inescapable. To do it right you'd have to live naked in a cave, hit your trout on the head with rocks, and eat them raw. But, so as not to violate another essential element of the fly-fishing tradition, the rocks would have to be quarried in England and cost $300 each.

Much of the inherent snootiness of fly-fishing begins to dissolve when you cease to specialize in the salmonids; the trout and salmon. Not only is it impossible to keep your nose in the air while fishing for bass or crappies, you're also in another culture where the value system is reversed. In trout fishing you'll find perfectly ordinary people trying to look, act, and sound like Old World sporting gentlemen, while on the bass ponds you'll run into doctors and lawyers making out like they quit school in the fourth grade to go work in the cotton fields. Bass writers even purposefully misspell words, like "hawg," while trout writers only misspell words by accident.

I may have been on the way to being a snob myself at one point. I was catching trout with some regularity on a split cane fly rod using flies I'd tied myself and was pretty self-satisfied. I'd learned just enough entomology to sound bewildering to those who didn't know any at all, and I guess I'll have to admit to feeling superior to spin fishermen, especially those who refused to be impressed by my language and my tackle.

Then I found out you could catch bass on a fly rod. Well, I guess I actually knew that all along, but when I read Dave Whitlock on the subject, it sounded neat. It also sounded familiar.

Species-specific trout purist or not, I was raised on bass, panfish, and pike, and five paragraphs into my first Whitlock article on bass bugging, I realized I missed them. I also realized the inherent possibilities in this: more fishing, more tackle, and more language—Southern English rather than Latin this time.

Back then, fly-fishing in warm water was not popular around here. Among the fly-casters I hung out with then (some of whom I still fish with) it was viewed with a kind of patient amusement. I was treated like the one guy in every crowd of beer drinkers who has a weak bladder.

My friend, Gil Lipp, who had at the time just decided that a nymph wasn't quite as bad as a live minnow, gave me the nickname that has, unfortunately, stuck for many years now: Grits. It was, of course, an allusion to Mr. Grits Gresham, one of the great outdoor writers who has become even more famous recently for his beer commercials on TV. That Gil even knew who Grits Gresham was revealed something of *his* hidden angling past (and he a native Colorado boy and all), but I let it pass.

To his credit, Gil soon started coming out with me in April

to catch spawning bluegills, rock bass, pumpkinseeds, and the occasional genuine largemouth bass. He pointed out that the rivers were in runoff and the dry-fly fishing for trout was lousy. He also insisted on using a 7½-foot, 4-weight split cane fly rod that he'd built himself. Intentional or not, that rod turned out to be an ideal tool for making the contest between fisherman and hand-sized bluegill a fair one.

At that time, Gil and I, and later A.K., were among the very few I ever saw waving fly rods on the local warm water ponds. Suddenly the vast majority of our colleagues were spin fishermen, and some of them really knew their stuff. I learned more from them than they did from me.

I also found that some of them were threading their grape-flavored rubber worms onto single, barbless hooks and were—wonder of wonders—releasing their fish.

Can you beat that?

More and more local fly-fishermen got into warm water—at about the same rate as its popularity was growing nationally—and it wasn't long before some of them called me to complain about the crimes being committed against the panfish in some local ponds by a small Vietnamese community. "They're hauling the fish out in buckets," they said, and hoped that, as the outdoor writer for a local newspaper, I could, "write it up, you know, get some action."

After a few phone calls and a little footwork, I came up with the following information:

A. None of these people were willing to risk their pending citizenship by getting busted for anything, least of all poaching fish.

B. They were keeping crappies, bluegills, and bullheads, and a legal combined limit for a family of five consisted of 400 fish, or "buckets" of them, if you prefer.

C. A fisheries biologist said that removing small panfish in those numbers (they kept everything they caught, no matter how small) could only help the overall gamefish population. That's why the limits were so generous in the first place.

D. The Vietnamese turned out to be friendly, polite, and damned good fishermen, putting many of us native Americans to shame on all three accounts.

And E. When you look into a bowl of Vietnamese fish stew, it looks back at you.

The people who called were right to be concerned, and more of us should call someone (even if it's only a reporter) when we think we see something wrong. But in this case it was a misunderstanding. Those guys were trouters who probably couldn't remember the last fish they'd killed.

As I said, things are a little different on warm water.

To some—to me, now—the purity of the sport is found nowhere but in the tackle. Because it's classy, demanding, and fun, you cast flies on a fly line and leader using a fly rod. Putting a fly ahead of a casting bubble on a spinning rod is effective in some situations, but it's not fly-fishing. Nymph fishing with a fly rod and a fly reel loaded with nothing but monofilament line is damned close, but it's not fly-fishing, either. Doing the same thing except with a fly line *is* fly-fishing because that's how I do it, and if it wasn't I'd have to give it up.

See?

Different species of fish in their different waters are all fair game, and each has its charms.

Taking trout on dry flies in flowing water is supreme if only because it's one of the loveliest things you'll ever have a hand in. It's better if the fly copies a real insect, even better if it's one you tied yourself, and better yet if it's one of your own design. Depending on how far you care to take it, it can be better still if you built the rod, tied the leader, and do it in a stream that no one else knows about.

Under some circumstances, one trout may be better than another. In the Mountain West, a cutthroat can be better than anything because it's a native. Same with the brook trout in the East. Rainbows can be better because they fight so nicely, while browns could be better because they're supposed to be smarter. A golden can be better just because it's so outrageous.

Big trout are better than little trout; difficult trout are better than either of the above; and big, difficult trout, well . . .

A huge trout caught on a streamer isn't as good as the same fish on a dry fly except if he's so big he doesn't eat winged insects anymore and so couldn't be caught that way. But then maybe he's in one of those glorious trout streams with 200 pounds of aquatic insects per acre of bottom and *does* still swallow a bug now and then. But then, you can never really be sure of that, can you?

There are very few things in life that are dead center. Three of them are: 1955 Ford pickups, B.B. King, and dry-fly fishing.

It's said that bass are smarter than trout because they'll eat something the like of which they haven't seen all week, "reasoning" that it's food. A trout, the same people say, is selective because he's too dumb to recognize anything but the little tan caddis flies he's eating at the moment as edible.

Whatever. Bass fishing with a fly rod can be delicate, careful stuff at times, but it never loses its inherent clunkiness. With more and more trout-fishers buying bass rods and fishing the ponds, bass flies are getting more realistic. As on the trout streams, fishermen will often answer the question, "What are you using?" by describing the creature they're trying to imitate: frog, leech, mouse, baby muskrat. But even the supposedly accurate patterns retain a bug-eyed goofiness, and those red and white things with the rubber legs that don't look like anything in nature are still much in evidence.

The hotshot, tournament-style bass-fishers use all kinds of electronic fish-finding gear and talk about pH factors, thermoclines, and other technical-sounding stuff. Many even treat their lures with chemical concoctions designed to put fish in a "positive feeding mood." One of the most popular of these is Dr. Juice Fish Scent. Dr. Juice himself is pictured on the label, and he looks like he's been drinking the stuff. He also looks a lot like the poet Allen Ginsburg, but I'm sure that's just a coincidence.

Fly-fishers, on the other hand, tend to retain a pastoral attitude. They cast their deer hair bugs along the weed beds in the evenings with little thought of the water chemistry. "Twitch it once and then just let it sit there," they say. "Drives bass nuts."

Panfish look and act like little bass (they're in the same family, after all) and function as the fish that even serious anglers don't have to take seriously if they don't feel like it. The big ones are not that easy to find, but you can almost always catch the average fish, with a fly rod, without squinting your eyes, grinding your teeth, agonizing over what fly to use, or even thinking very hard. You can get intense about them if you want to, and you'll be rewarded for it, but they can also offer some relief in a discipline where trout, bass, and several other more "respectable" game fish must be taken seriously or not at all.

Panfish are also handsome fish, ranging from the tasteful, almost tweedy crappies to the gaudy pumpkinseeds, and you can keep a large limit of them without feeling the least bit guilty.

Pike are primordial-looking and have a threatening appearance that they can make good on. Their teeth are like needles, their gill covers are like knives, and the spines on their fins are like spikes. Guides often hate them because they lead to injuries, and experienced pike-fishers use long-handled hook disgorgers to handle them.

They're the only freshwater game fish I can think of that were named for a weapon of war.

In the right kind of water at least, the fly rod is as effective as any other kind of tackle, but very few fly patterns have been designed expressly for pike. Most use bass flies even though three or four big pike can shred a deer hair bug down to a bare hook. Real pike flies are usually simple—i.e., easy to replace—and durable. You can make a good one by wiring a strip of screaming yellow rabbit fur, skin and all, to a weighted hook.

Pike can be as low-spirited as largemouth bass in places where they're heavily fished, but the few wild ones I've caught, in the Northwest Territories and, years ago, in northern Minnesota, had the confident aggressiveness of animals that aren't used to being messed with.

Once, in Canada, we were fishing for pike in a narrow channel between two lakes. The place was known to the guides as the Snake River because it looked a little like a river and was full of pike, or "snakes," as they called them with obvious distaste. Both sides of the channel were lined with deep weed beds that could be twenty feet wide. You'd slap a popper on the outside edge, and the stalks would begin to part five feet back as a big pike with blood in his eye charged out. With this kind of warning it was easy to strike too soon and miss the fish, but it didn't matter. Cast the popper back out and he'd come for it again.

We were doing this with fairly light tackle—7-weight fly rods with about 6-pound leader tippets—and the fish could have broken us off easily by simply diving back into the obvious safety of the weeds, as any bass or trout I've ever caught could be expected to do. But not a one did. They fought hard, but they did it out in the open water where they didn't have a chance unless they inadvertently rolled up in your leader and cut it with their sharp gill covers. This is the innocence you see in truly wild things that still think people can be dealt with in the same way as other predators. It's the same mistake once made by the American bison and the passenger pigeon, and, although we were happily catching lots of big fish, it was ever so slightly heartbreaking.

But we *were* catching big fish and it never once occurred to us to reel in and go home. A fisherman's sympathy always comes later, after the fact.

Fly-fishing for trout is poetic; for bass it's somewhat existential; for panfish it's corny, but fun. For pike it's rough and tumble— the branch of the sport that reminds me of stock car racing.

To some, this business of doing things right translates as flying first class, you know, up in the front of the plane where the seats are wider and you get your drinks before the folks back in steerage do. Excuse me, "cocktails." These are the fishermen who make the distinction between drinks and cocktails; between the camp cook and the chef at the lodge. They spend a good deal of money.

There's nothing wrong with this unless, like the snob, having the best gets you to thinking you deserve it.

I have very little experience with this kind of fishing. I'm your standard proletarian, drive all night, sleep in a tent, cook off the tailgate kind of fisherman. For both esthetic and practical reasons, I go in what Thomas McGuane would call the style of the "Old Rugged." It's an important distinction here in the West. According to McGuane, the *New* Rugged consists of working on screenplays so the bank doesn't take the ranch.

The only experience I've had with upper crust fly-fishing was a few years ago at Three Rivers Ranch on the Henry's Fork.

The lodge was old and rustic in a purposeful way. Not phony, just carefully orchestrated. I found it seductively comfortable; a place where you could easily lounge around in leather chairs talking fishing until the wee hours while sipping good whiskey served from an elaborately carved oak bar. Or maybe it was mahogany.

I stayed in a two-bedroom cabin—one of several—that was furnished with antiques, including an ornate potbelly stove with one of those chrome loving cups on top. Plenty of hot water, towels, the beds changed daily, and a chilled bottle of white wine and a bowl of fresh fruit waiting when I checked in.

There was a small Orvis shop on the premises which did not appear to be open to the public.

I fished with two of the guides and found them to be somewhat older than most in the area, at least as good, if not better than average, and noticeably more solicitous to sports.

Now, don't get the idea I paid for this. A full-blown week at Three Rivers would have cost me what I normally spend on a half a year's fishing. I was graciously invited to slip in for a few days before the real paying guests arrived; while the guides were still scoping the rivers and the chef was trying out some new dishes.

I wasn't uncomfortable. In fact, I was more comfortable than I'd ever been before on a fishing trip. It became evident that, given the chance, I could get spoiled easily. Still, I felt vaguely out of my element.

The first day I floated the lower Henry's Fork from Warm River down past Ashton with Dennis Bitton and one of the guides. The fishing was good, but that's not what I recall. We were back in time for drinks and then a fine meal; the kind that comes with several forks, and I learned that, although one doesn't exactly dress for dinner, one at least puts on a clean shirt.

The next afternoon a guide and I ended up on a remote stretch of Robinson Creek—one of the great underrated streams in that part of the country. We slogged down into a steep canyon and caught a few nice brown trout on nymphs. Slow fishing, but good. Then, as evening came on, a hatch of small, wheat-colored caddis flies came off and fish began to rise. I tried a #16 Elk Hair dry which the fish refused, and was just switching to a #18 when my guide came over and said, "I should mention that even if we leave now we'll still be late for cocktails."

In all my years of fishing, no one had ever said anything like that to me before.

I'm one of those fly-fishers who do actually take panfish—bluegills in particular—seriously. I scout their spawning runs in the spring, try my best to plot their population cycles, and otherwise maintain a fascination for them. In recent years I've taken to fishing for them with an 8½-foot, 2-weight graphite rod that I've reserved exclusively for panfish ever since I discovered that I could cast a #6 or #8 popper with it. A quarter-pound bluegill will bend it double, and I once landed a 4-pound bass with it by accident, but that's another story.

I think bluegills are best fished for with long, light rods that let them show off, so when I came across a magazine ad for telescoping crappie rods, I got an idea. These things are 11 to 15 feet long, very whippy, and not all that bad looking. And, the ad said, some are designed to be used with a fly line and bugs. Generically they're crappie rods, but the various models have names like "Bream Buster" and "Perch Jerker." It was too much to resist.

I ordered one straight from Alabama and have been watching the highway for the UPS truck ever since. The man I talked to on the phone couldn't tell me about line weights, but said the rods were real noodly. Maybe I can get away with a 2- or 3-weight line.

When I asked what kind of reel seats the rods had, the guy said, "They don't *have* reel seats, but some people tape reels to the handles."

Fine. Why not?

·

Home
Water

·

Rivers.

If you say "South Platte," in the circles I travel in, you probably mean the catch-and-release water in Cheesman Canyon. If you mean the stretch between Deckers and Trumbull, you have to specify that. Say "Frying Pan," and you mean the part below Ruedi Dam. "The River" becomes synonymous with where you fish it, so that, although I know better, I can't help thinking of the Platte as being about ten miles long and the Pan as more like four or five. When I fish somewhere else on these drainages, the connection is more intellectual than real. I'm unable to grasp the enormousness of it.

And a river *is* enormous. On a map it looks as complex and organic as the roots of a tree, sucking its livelihood from every possible crack in what passes for soil in the mountains. Start adding up the tributaries and you can get hundreds of miles of flowing water just in the headwaters. Looking farther upstream, you see trickles too small to have either names or fish, and then snow, and then global weather.

Look downstream and you'll see larger and larger rivers, then oceans, and then the tugging of the moon on the tides.

It's a huge, dizzying cycle almost too big to comprehend, and it comes to you only in the occasional dumbstruck moment when the fish aren't biting and your mind wanders. But don't feel badly. To a trout, "The River" is a hole behind a rock.

Of all the rivers I've fished, the one I've seen the most of is the St. Vrain. It's a small one—some prefer to call it a creek, and it's hard to argue—that's one of the major feeders of the South Platte. My own hole behind a rock is the three-quarter-mile stretch of the main branch that flows in front of the house here, but upstream from that are more than 300 miles of forks and feeder streams draining several hundred square miles of the northern Colorado Rockies. Rough figures, of course. It's a big chunk of land slopping over several artificial boundaries: from Roosevelt National Forest to the Indian Peaks Wilderness Area to Rocky Mountain National Park.

If you get out the U.S. Geologic Survey maps covering the drainage and put them all together, they cover the living room floor. Over there by the woodstove you can see the blue bead-chain of headwater lakes strung along a jagged north/south line, each one hung in the first level spot the water comes to as it runs off the Continental Divide, flowing east, or toward the bathroom. A few of these lakes still don't have official names, which delights me. They're called differently by different fishermen, so that Keith's Pond and Boy Scout Lake are really the same, although on the map it's just one of several anonymous blue spots—the one with the brook trout in it.

There are three major forks of the St. Vrain which are called, simply and eloquently, the North, Middle, and South, plus a half-dozen or so important feeder creeks. The South and Middle forks come together a few miles up the South canyon from here, and then that stream has its confluence with the North Fork up the road in the little town of Lyons, a pleasant and fairly quiet little burg built square in the flood plain on the first available piece of level real estate.

The main branch is short-lived as a trout stream. By the time it's gotten very far out onto the plains it's been drained for irrigation, polluted by agriculture, bulldozed, and otherwise trashed by the people who see streams as nothing more than ditches for "their" water. You have to watch out for people like that. They're wrong in the beginning, but they can become right; given half a chance, they'll turn a river *into* a ditch.

At the highest elevations it's real postcard stuff: incredible craggy peaks with snow, boulder fields, and mossy-looking patches of alpine tundra sloping down to lovely, small, trout lakes, any one of which would look fine on a liquor store calendar.

The scenic shots you see are all taken on calm, blue days with wide-angle lenses, and they only look magnificent. The real, teeth-rattling beauty of the Indian Peaks high country shows itself during storms when the John Denver song lyrics are replaced by a hint of the survival situation; the suspicion that the smart humans are back in town sipping cold beers. Once last summer and once the summer before, I had to build quick fires on the east slope of the Indian Peaks Wilderness Area (where fires are prohibited now) because I was cold and wet and one hell of a long way from the truck. I'd like to take this opportunity to turn myself in.

It should go without saying that the lakes tend to fish best in foul weather.

This is wet country, even though the climate is considered semiarid. That's because so much of the state's moisture falls as snow and rain in the high country and then runs downhill. The soil is loose and rocky with good drainage, so the ridges are dry, but the low spots can be marshy, and such things as ferns and even mushrooms sometimes grow. The spruces and firs along the tree line are often stunted and flagged, but give them a little shelter from the wind and they'll grow tall and straight.

In other words, the countryside changes around every bend. There are some ridges with so many downed trees it can take you an hour to pick through a hundred yards of it, and up near the tree line the boulder fields can also be slow going. You just plain stay off the scree slopes, even if it means a long detour. Scree slopes were made for French existentialists: for every step up you slide two down—and your boots fill with gravel.

Down in the trees the going is mostly open and easy with very little underbrush, and there are places where you can hike for miles on the level, once you get up there. In some areas, the only impediment is altitude. Up near the Divide where the pitch gets severe there are ponds hung in preposterous places. One of them is sometimes referred to as Bust a Gut Lake.

Up here, the best fishing is in the lakes themselves. The streams are small and so, usually, are their trout, but there are always exceptions. Good-sized trout do turn up, sometimes in surprising places, and this keeps you going, wondering what that stretch of Mitchell Creek between here and there looks like. Sometimes the only way to find out is to bushwhack in and see for yourself. The established trails go unerringly to the popular lakes, while the streams wander around by themselves, undisturbed and under-fished for many miles.

I've been kicking around in this area for about seventeen years now, mostly with a fly rod, sometimes with a rifle or shotgun, and now and then with just a walking stick and a pair of binoculars. If all the miles I'd walked were laid end to end, I'd have seen the river's entire headwater drainage about twice. As it is, I've seen less than half of it.

Fishing the whole thing, say, from my house up all the forks and feeders to the various points where trout are no longer found, is a kind of idle goal. Maybe I'll do it, maybe I won't. The trouble is, when you find a secret little meadow where the stream is deep and the trout are large, you have to go back, right?

This chunk of the Rocky Mountains is a model of many ecological zones. At the highest elevations, you're in alpine tundra, the kind of landscape you'll see above the northern tree line way up at the top of the Northwest Territories. Downhill from that you have various types of forests until, at the base of the foothills, you run into the first deciduous trees. Walk five miles east and you're in high plains desert where you can't wear tennis shoes because the spikes of the prickly pear cactus will go through the canvas. There are places around here where you can take a forty-mile hike that, on level ground, would amount to walking from northern New Mexico to the Arctic Circle.

The water itself, being the most passive of elements, happily takes on the character of the country it runs through—fast, slow, deep, shallow, whatever you want—and the trout are very much like the water. They're numerous or few, they grow big or stay small, as conditions dictate. They do exactly what they're supposed to, no more, no less.

Up high, you'll find mostly cutthroats and brook trout along with some rainbows and rainbow/cutthroat hybrids. Somewhat farther down you get into the browns and more rainbows. On the North and Middle forks you can find the places where the guard changes—the stretch of a mile or so where you can take all four species in a single afternoon. The grand slam. These spots seem to slide around a bit, being a little higher one year and a little lower the next, for reasons of their own.

The South Fork would have a place like that, too, except that one of the more accessible headwater lakes is stocked regularly with what the Division of Wildlife likes to call "catchable-sized" rainbows that naturally dribble out into the South Fork downstream. Above that, the Division has stocked Emerald Lake rainbows, a fertile rainbow/cutthroat cross that reproduces well and grows large in mountain lakes.

The upper lakes used to have brook trout in them, but those were poisoned out to make room for the Emerald Lake fish. Some have problems with that and others don't. I sort of miss the brookies myself, but then the new fish are harder to catch and bigger (which probably makes them "better" in the high-brow sporting sense), and the brookies weren't native, either, although they were definitely home grown.

Yes, it's been tampered with, there and in other places, sometimes for the better and sometimes for the worse.

The St. Vrain is ideal home water for me precisely because there's a lot of it and most of it is somewhere between average and fair-to-middling, or "good enough for who it's for," as one local angler puts it. You can fish it with deadly seriousness or casually, depending on how you feel at the moment, simply because the trout are not typically large. Anywhere on it, a 12-incher is a pretty good one.

That's not to say it's easy. It can be, but it can also be so difficult that this reporter can't catch fish at all. You'd have to say that the St. Vrain is a moody little sucker. It has the irritating tendency to hatch what would be its best bugs—the big Golden Stones, Green Drake and Gray Drake mayflies—in the early spring when the river is muddy and fly-fishing is largely out of the question, and then be stingy with its insects during the daylight hours of summer and fall. But then, just to show you what it could be like if it ever got clockwork regular like the Henry's Fork, one afternoon it will send you a good Blue-winged Olive hatch and then a masking caddis hatch and then a Red Quill spinner fall as if to say, "I can do it if I want to, I just usually don't feel like it."

And then there are the days when it decides to hide all its fish and does it so well that, if you didn't know better, you'd swear there wasn't a trout left anywhere.

I'm not a counter, so I have no idea how many days I've fished the St. Vrain or how many of its trout I've caught, even in the decade since I've lived within sight of it. Possibly not as many of either as I'd like to think. I do know that when I inherited enough money to buy a cheap old house, I knew what stream I wanted it to be on.

Now I've fished in a number of places over the years, and there are few things I love more than the adventure of wading into a new river for the first time or finding a new mountain lake. Still, the home water infiltrates your consciousness in a distinctive and comfortable way. It becomes an inescapable part of daily life.

The little town of Lyons, although it has a trout stream running right through it, isn't what you'd call a fishing community. You can buy worms at the grocery store, and the muzzleloading gun shop sells genuine A.K. Best trout flies, but that's about it. Taken as a group, local sportsmen are more into elk than trout.

On the other hand, just about everyone has fished the river—because it's there. Many do it the way they always have, using the same fly patterns or baits their daddies showed them thirty and forty years ago and keeping the same number of trout, regardless of the changes in regulations that have come and gone. These guys seem as unmovable as forces of nature; their behavior as predetermined as that of the trout themselves. Outside forces wash over them and they go from being legal fishermen one year to poachers the next without seeming to notice.

In a way they're kind of charming, and they could be at least partially forgiven except that they're teaching the same ethic to the next generation:

Fishing lesson #1. "First, keep an eye out for the ranger. Now, grasp the rod firmly in your right hand . . ."

I don't like poachers and I don't poach myself—now—although I must admit that in my misspent youth I did step over the line a time or two. I believe the statute of limitations has now run out on those offenses. I yell at poachers when I catch them, but not as loudly as I used to. I mean, I do have to live here.

The first summer the catch-and-release regulations were on I stumbled upon three guys fishing live hoppers and keeping fish. I was righteously pissed and, feeling that my strength was as the strength of ten because my heart was pure, I waded in. I read them my best riot act and they listened attentively. Too attentively, in fact. Their eyes were cold and level and they began to flex the sinues in their yard-wide shoulders. Jaw muscles twitched ominously. Halfway through my spiel I began to think, "This had better be good because it's probably the last speech I'll ever give. When I stop for a breath, these three twenty-year-old stone masons are gonna kill me."

They didn't, but only because they weren't in the mood. It wouldn't have been amusing enough to bother with.

Once you become known as a fisherman around here, you can't walk down the street or buy a cup of coffee without being asked about, or told about, fishing. Most no longer recount their illegal exploits to me because they know where I stand. They also know that Colorado now has a Game Thief program where you can turn poachers in for a reward. A bad fisherman pays less than half of what a bad big game hunter is worth ($100 as opposed to $250), but it's still a fair piece of change. I've never done it because this is a small town where feuds are a major source of diversion, especially in the winter when things are slow, and where a certain frontier mentality persists. It's not the kind of place where you can lightly date someone's wife or call the heat on a neighbor.

Still, the temptation exists. (I'm talking about the reward, of course.)

To be fair, it's better now than it once was. This conservation business has a logic to it that's inescapable, and I like to think we fly-fishing types (or outsiders or whippersnappers if you prefer) have had some effect. If nothing else, the remaining poachers are sneaking and hiding more than they used to. Then again, there are fewer restrictions to obey now than there once were, but more on that later.

I was married for a while out here—to the second and, perhaps, last wife of my career—but it didn't last long. There we were, out in the country where wild animals lived; where people carried rifles in their pickup trucks; where vast tracts of vegetation remained unmowed. We were too far from the bright lights. (Lyons does, by the way, have some bright lights, but all but the two traffic signals tend to go out around nine o'clock most nights.)

She once asked, "Why the hell are all these middle-aged men sitting around doing nothing?" To which I answered, "You have a very citified idea of what 'doing *something*' means."

And then there was the endless fishing, and all the *talk* about fishing. I thought it was great, she thought it was shitty—boring—corny.

As Norman McClean might have said, the river sort of ran through all this. It seemed to tell me, in a dozen subtle ways per day, that you can't have two things at once if those two things cancel each other out and, further, that you should probably choose the one that has never gone out of its way to screw you around.

I remember the summer afternoon when Ex-Wife and I had what was to be our last civil conversation. We were sitting in the outside patio of the Black Bear Inn—which has since been enclosed for use in the winter. The Black Bear is across the street from the river, and, between cars, I could hear the current. When a #16 Red Quill spinner landed on the lip of my gin and tonic glass, it all became clear: this conversation would have to end in time for me to make the evening spinner fall which, to be safe, gave us about half an hour.

Have you ever noticed how when one thing becomes clear,

everything else goes down like dominoes? How the answer is found in nothing more than a consise statement of the question?

She was leaving.

I was staying.

Now, was that a size 16 or maybe a 14?

Of course, those of us who fish the St. Vrain regularly have the obligatory "Legend of the Twenty-Inch Trout." Like all such legends on otherwise mediocre streams, it is based on—but not bound by—fact.

The first big trout I saw on the St. Vrain was a brown, but then they're all browns—both the ones we've seen and the ones we haven't. That's because it's the brown trout who has the nocturnal nature, the sullen stubbornness, and the appetite for fish, ducklings, and small rodents that lets him find a quiet corner where he can secretly grow to the size of a torpedo unnoticed even by the locals.

In those days, "The St. Vrain" was synonymous with the first mile or so of the main branch below Lyons, the place where the forks come shooting down from their rocky, pine-forested canyons to suddenly find themselves flowing slowly over more or less level ground between stands of leafy trees. It was probably the best single mile on the whole stream and also about the last of the trout fishing.

I was out with Gil and we were fishing dry flies. That is, we would *have* to have been fishing dry flies because Gil, in those days, at least, would fish with nothing else. Nymphs and streamers "might as well be bait." Judging from the season, I'll guess the hatch was either Light Cahills or Red Quills, not heavy, but enough to keep the fish looking up.

I had caught a few trout and was hiking back downstream to see how Gil was doing. I found him casting to a pod of risers below a diversion dam, so I sat down on the edge of the concrete abutment to watch. The water was down and clear and the light was good. I spotted the fish Gil was casting to—about a 9- or 10-inch brown, rising steadily—and then one or two others above that. And then . . . . Naw, that can't be a trout, it's two feet long.

But if it wasn't a trout, it was doing a hell of a good imitation; finning quietly at the edge of the current, rising without a discernible rhythm to the little mayflies. The disturbance it made on the surface was no more than that of the smaller fish, but the bubbles it left were as big around as silver dollars.

Gil and I were just out of voice range, so I waved for his attention and, in sign language, tried to tell him about the size of the trout and its location. He shrugged. I went through the performance again, and Gil signed back, very clearly, that I'd been out in the sun too long without a hat.

So I pointed and yelled as loudly as I could over the noise of the stream, "Enormous trout right there, you (deleted) idiot!"

He understood. He looked. He looked for a long time, and when he finally saw it, he tensed into the posture of a man about to run from a bear.

I watched as he worked into position and made a beautiful cast that went right where it should have and settled the dry fly delicately on the water. At which point the trout vanished into the deep water, leaving behind it a boil the size of a spare tire that rippled down into the current and also disappeared.

Neither of us ever caught that fish or even saw him again, but we know he came to a bad end.

Only a few weeks later one of the ditch companies dumped a dose of algicide into their ditch to clean out the vegetation. It did a nice job on the cement-sided channel, and it did a job on the river, too, below where the irrigation water emptied into the main branch. According to the health department report, 1,395 brown trout were found dead along two miles of stream along with 453 fish of "other species," that is, suckers and dace. Several of those trout were 20 inches or better. Not one, *several*.

No one seemed to know what this had done to the insect population, except that there were still bugs under the rocks. But then, in September, the Blue-winged Olives came off as usual, a good heavy hatch, bank to bank, with nary a rise. I walked over and watched it for a few days running and then couldn't take it anymore. You know that feeling you can get that stretches from abject sadness on one end to purple rage on the other? You don't know whether to cry or go get the deer rifle and kill someone, so you just sit there, steaming like a fresh cow pie.

For me—a fairly young, conservation-minded, divorced, reconfirmed dry-fly fishing bachelor freelance writer with a part-time job—it was the year the universe swung several more degrees to the left.

I joined up with a disparate group of local anglers who were also teetering between sadness and rage to form a chapter of Trout Unlimited with the express purpose of "doing something" about the St. Vrain. I ended up on the board of directors where I stayed for five years, shuttling from one office to another and narrowly escaping the presidency several times. I didn't want to be president, and my excuse was that whoever held that position should have a cooler head than mine. They didn't have to agree with me as easily as they did.

"Yeah," they'd say, "I guess you're right."

Over the next five years, the following things happened:

We lobbied the Division of Wildlife, the Wildlife Commission, and anyone else who'd listen asking for special regulations on the main branch, preferably catch and release.

About two years later, no-kill regulations did, in fact, go into effect on the main branch of the river.

Then we started the whole process all over again trying to get money to rebuild the fish habitat in that stretch.

The Division gave us $15,000, and we got a rough blueprint (for free) from a graduate student in fisheries biology.

We rebuilt the habitat, or at least we moved a lot of rocks around at great expense.

That, naturally, is a very brief account. It doesn't reflect the endless, maddening hassles: the D.O.W. biologist who told us, "Shoot, you guys want trout? You tell us where you want 'em, we'll bring you a truckload"; the landowners along the river who wouldn't sign a lease for public access until they had a million dollars worth of liability insurance; and two dozen other festering problems that I don't care to remember and you probably don't care to hear about, either.

We pulled it off, finally, largely through sheer brute strength and ignorance, but several of us burned out rather badly before it was all over. A righteous cause can do that to you. You fight the spoilers of trout streams and then sometimes you have to turn around and fight your own organization as well, either because they're wrong, or you're wrong, or just because you drive a Ford and they all drive Chevies—or, in this case, BMWs.

We were, after all, young, mostly blue collar, and idealistic (prime candidates for some serious disillusionment). We were also a small, radical chapter on an equally small trout stream that was a long way from the Mother Church in Denver. At best, we had a fuzzy vision of the big picture, and the phrase "political realities" came to sound to us like fingernails on a blackboard. To us, political realities meant that the right thing was obvious, but that the *wrong* thing was going to be done because some bastard—or group of bastards—would benefit from it.

We were going to change that, of course, and those of us who seemed to run things for a while (the Lyons Mafia, we were called) managed to rattle a number of cages in the process. It was a difficult time, during which some of us learned something about reality—political and otherwise.

The river itself seemed oddly unconcerned with all this. While we were lobbying and arguing, the main branch quietly reseeded itself with trout from the healthy upper forks. New fish took up residence more or less in the same places the old ones had lived, and three years after the fish kill, A.K. hooked what he described as a 20-inch trout at a place known as the Rock Pool. He didn't land the fish. Instead he got back his #16 Rusty Spinner with the hook bent straight.

That was the summer A.K. came out here from Michigan, where he was a public school band director and part-time flytier, to work for three months in a fly shop. It was also the year we met and began our long, weird, rollicking friendship. In fact, he hooked that fish on his last night in town. He'd been staying with Ken Iwamasa, but Ken wasn't home when A.K. left. So, by way of a farewell note, he stuck the bent fly in Ken's vise and went back to Alpena. The following spring, he showed up with his family and has been here ever since.

The river was coming back nicely, but it was being fished more than ever before because of the increased attention it was getting. When the catch-and-release regulations went on, the fishing pressure doubled overnight. Stories of excessive numbers of large trout being caught began to circulate, and that brought even more fly-fishermen.

I'll have to say that most of those stories were untrue. For a period of a few years, it was easy enough to find a fisherman who claimed he'd taken several dozen 16- to 18-inch browns from the catch-and-release section in a single summer, while the biologists' reports said there were virtually *no* trout in there over 14 inches long, and not too many of those.

Rather than suggest those guys were lying, let's just assume their judgement was clouded by their expectations.

The 20-inch trout legend continued, of course, and there was, in fact, a sounder scientific basis for it than there is for, say, the Loch Ness Monster.

Just before the catch-and-release regulations went on, there was an electro-shocking survey done on two 100-meter stretches of the main branch. It was one of several such things that were done regularly up until a few years ago when the biologists figured they'd learned all there was to know about that particular trout population, packed up their equipment, and drove away.

If you've never helped with an electro-shocking survey, you should do it sometime, just for the experience. On shore you have a small generator making electricity. Out in the water you have a dozen or so people in waders. Some are holding electrodes and the rest are holding large dip nets. The electrodes are connected to the generator by long wires. The idea is to send a mild current into the water that stuns the trout just long enough for them to be netted and placed into a live box. They are then weighed, measured, and scale samples are taken. From this data, the biologists can figure out all kinds of things for sure and infer some other things, like what effect special regulations have on the trout population.

It's a lot of fun, but it can also be disturbing to see an old familiar stream laid open like that. Whatever you thought you knew about it, chances are you were wrong. Worse yet, the fabulous mystery of it will never quite be the same again.

But it *is* fun.

As we charged through the Rock Pool, the head biologist spotted a brown that he later described as "a good 20 inches." Losing his scientific detachment for a few seconds, he yelled, "Get that big son of a bitch, boy oh boy oh boy!"

Well, we didn't get him, but most of us saw him. It had to be the one that had bent A.K.'s hook straight.

During another shocking survey at yet another spot, we did get the big one, and he ended up weighing eight pounds. These fish are known to the biologists as statistical anomalies and are not included in the final results because they would skew the numbers, making the "average" trout bigger than he really was. The biologists aren't surprised at these fish. "Any healthy brown trout stream has a couple of monsters," they say. A fact to the scientist, an article of faith to the fisherman.

But the fact remained that, for all the regulations, habitat work, and studies, the biggest fish in the catch-and-release area were, for all practical purposes, about 14 inches long. And, in fact, the *average* trout was more like 8 or 9. With, of course, the occasional submarine.

In other words, the river was pretty much like it had always been, except that it had cost the D.O.W. $15,000, the local volunteers five years worth of time and effort, and had been fished in by more people in three years than it had seen in the last fifty.

Some said the big fish were swimming out the irrigation ditches and dying, others said they were being taken out by dastardly bait-fishing poachers at night, and so on. Put a group of fly-fishers on a problem and you'll get more theories than you know what to do with. Finally a fisheries biologist named Anderson told me he thought he had it. "Stream flow," he said. "There's so little water in here in the winter that a trout bigger than about 13 or 14 inches doesn't have deep enough water to survive in. Little fish can make it in shallow water, but not the big ones."

And what about the few hogs?

"Look where they come from," he said. "The only deep holes

in the entire stretch. Now, if you had a minimum flow of about 30 cubic feet per second, you'd really have something."

The mistake turned up at the bottom of a five-year-deep stack of documents. The plan drawn up by the fisheries biologist had, in fact, been based on a minimum winter flow of around 30 c.f.s. About half of that water was supposed to come sluicing down the river from Button Rock Dam on the North Fork on its way to cool the reactors of a nuclear power plant out on the plains. But the power plant never worked, and so it didn't get hot, and so it didn't have to be cooled, and so the water was never released. The thing hasn't worked to this day. They're still tinkering with it, but when they start it up it sputters and backfires like a thirty-year-old pickup and then stops again. I'm not the only one around here who believes the thing will never work.

The Division of Wildlife dropped the catch-and-release regulations because, in the words of one official, "We weren't getting what we wanted out of it." There was talk of making it Wild Trout Water, a designation that would have carried a two-fish limit and a flies-and-lures-only restriction, but that never happened and no one argued. The Division walked away, T.U. walked away, and the hordes of eager fly-fishers left, shaking their heads and spouting their theories, many of them firmly convinced that they'd been catching 16- to 18-inch brown trout that had suddenly and inexplicably vanished.

There were a few seasons in there when I hardly fished the catch-and-release water at all. It was too crowded, my favorite places were always taken by strangers, and some of my favorite places weren't even there anymore—we'd improved them out of existence with the bulldozer.

I fished more in the headwaters then, discovering new spots, rediscovering old ones, catching trout sometimes with whole lakes cluttered by no one except me and whoever I was with. The mountains are getting crowded these days, especially in the more accessible parts of the wilderness area and the national park, but there are still corners of both that are nice and lonely. I've still never made it to Bust a Gut Lake. I'm waiting for someone to tell me there are fish there first.

Now, with the fishing pressure down and the catch-and-release regulations lifted, the main branch of the St. Vrain is slowly coming back to what it was in the years before the fish kill. The trout continue to struggle with the low winter flows, but they maintain, and, the ethics of the sport notwithstanding, it doesn't hurt to eat a few keepers that probably won't make it through the winter anyway.

The guys who were poachers just a few years ago are legal again, except on those days when they go over the eight-fish limit.

You'll see a few new faces now, but many of the fly-fishers have vanished as completely as those mythical 18-inch browns. New streams have become fashionable, and there are new projects that have been more successful in terms of growing bushels of big trout and attracting enough fly-fishermen to cause parking problems. Those projects all have one thing in common; they have water.

I've heard the St. Vrain catch-and-release project called a failure and a tragedy, and it might be both, depending on how you choose to look at it. On the other hand, it's less than a mile of stream out of over 300; a stretch of civilized water that we humans first wrecked, then tried to fix, and that is at least no worse off now than it was before we started. All that stream work wasn't for nought, either. Ken Iwamasa, who has been studying the insects in the main branch for years, says there are noticeably more bugs in there now than before the project. He thinks it has to do with the increased surface area on the bottom that resulted from all that rattling around with the heavy equipment.

And at least we now have a few T.U. members around to keep an eye on things. This is, after all, the end of the twentieth century, and leaving even a little trout stream unwatched is like leaving your wallet on the bar while you go to the bathroom: it *might* be there when you get back, but if it's not, it's your own damn fault.

A few more people fish the main branch than fished it a decade ago—but not a lot more, considering—and otherwise it's just about back to the way it was before: a modest, sleepy little trout stream that's plenty good enough for who it's for.

•

THE
UPSIDE
DOWN
WEEDLESS
ROCK
KNOCKER

•

I don't exactly remember the first time I met Ken Iwamasa, but it was probably in the old Western Angler fly shop in Boulder, Colorado, a place where I sometimes worked, sometimes just hung around, and where customers were hard-pressed to tell the difference. I do, however, remember the first time I saw him.

I was fishing on the main branch of the St. Vrain near my house. It was sometime in that fraction of a season that comes between fall and winter and has elements of both. The river was low and clear, and the sky was the crisp, brilliant blue you get at the higher altitudes that suggests the proximity of outer space rather than a safe dome of atmosphere. The fishing was about as hard as it gets: the occasional brown trout rose lazily to the occasional size 24 midge—stalking and crouching to keep your shadow off the water; fishing the longest, finest leader you could manage; trying to wade in the nearly still water without making ripples, spooking a whole pool with a single cast, that sort of thing.

If memory serves me, I was not catching fish and was probably telling myself it was good practice, like jogging in ankle weights or some other form of self-abuse. I was alone on the river, and that was pleasant, although it might have meant that every other fly-fisherman I knew was smarter than I was.

At least I thought I was alone.

I first heard the laughter while I was back in the trees away from the water, taking a shortcut in the direction of the place known to some as Walsh Riffle.

It's a fine little woods in there, nestled in the transition zone where the foothills have almost given way to the plains, where the coniferous forests of the mountains begin to turn into deciduous groves. On the valley rim are ponderosa pines, while down in the bottomland along the river are what pass for hardwoods in the Mountain West: willow, cottonwood, box elder. If you go quietly through there—at less than the normal human get-there-and-the-hell-with-the-scenery pace—you'll see lots of birds and maybe some deer.

So there I was, almost sneaking along, assuming I was alone, when I heard laughing. At first my brain wanted to make it into a bird call (a cock pheasant!) but no, it was clearly a person being amused at something.

Then I really did sneak, over to the river where I peeked through the bushes and saw a slightly built Oriental gentleman kneeling on the gravel, playing a modest-sized trout and giggling happily to himself.

My first impulse was to walk out there and ask the time-honored question that occurs to the man who is not catching fish: "What did you get him on?" but then I realized, just in time, that only an insensitive clod would intrude on such a scene.

And anyway, in a situation like that the question isn't so much "What did you get him on?" as it is *"How?"*

I gave up and went home then. It had been an afternoon of fishing where catching a single trout—or maybe even just getting a strike—would have counted as a victory. If anyone had asked if I'd taken any fish that day, I would have said, "No, but I think I saw a woodland spirit."

It was a pretty scene—the kind of thing that sticks in your mind as a slice of what fishing is all about, one of those times when esthetics outweighs success. It's also a kind of character study of the type of person who not only ties beautiful flies, but also invents patterns that, as they say, "enter the literature of the sport." These are the people who still impress the hell out of me.

When I first started tying, it was in imitation of the great fly-tiers, which seems to be typical. As Kurt Vonnegut recently pointed out, we're the only animals with brains big enough to let us enjoy things that not only haven't happened yet, but that may *never* happen. When my big brain took up fly tying, it focused on the unattainable heights, leaving my poor soul to wade through all the crap it would take to get anywhere close.

To be fair, the brain did help out with some prodding and an ingenious string of rationalizations.

After that, I talked with Ken at the fly shop and ran into him often on the St. Vrain. He especially liked it in the fall when the flies were tiny and the fishing was hard. He parked his car where I could see it from the front porch, and I'd sometimes walk over to see how he was doing. On other occasions I'd literally stumble on him as he knelt or even sprawled on the bank working an agonizingly long drift down to a single rising trout.

Ken has always fascinated me because he somehow manages to balance the two paradoxical elements that make a great fisherman. He's relentless, but also slow paced and good humored. He's an artist and teacher by trade and is also an adventurous and original inventor of fly patterns. Definitely the kind of man you want haunting your home water.

He's well known for his fly patterns, some of which have gained national popularity. One you may have seen is the Iwamasa Dun, the dry mayfly pattern with the split tails, dubbed body with a deer hair shell back, upright wings burned to the proper silhouette with a wing burner of Ken's own design, and sparse deer hair legs. It's a mayfly pattern that actually looks like a mayfly, rather than just suggesting one as most do, and it comes from the most obvious kind of logic. "If you can tell the difference between your fly and the natural at thirty yards," Ken once said, "just think of what the trout sees."

It's a beautiful fly, and it's one of the few attempts at a starkly realistic imitation of a mayfly dun I've seen that really works. You have to be within inches to tell it from the real thing. It also illustrates the ability that only a very few flytiers have to be able to look at a common trout stream insect as though they'd never seen one before and then reinvent it at the vise.

At the time it first appeared, there was nothing quite like it, although there are now some similar patterns floating around. Similar, but not exact, and fine distinctions can count for a lot. Fly tying is, after all, an exercise in splitting hairs (no pun intended). At this writing, the Iwamasa Dun is only available from the maestro himself, on a custom basis.

Another one you may have seen is the Tarcher Nymph, a mayfly nymph pattern tied upside down on an English bait hook so that it swims upside down, making it nearly weedless and also imitating the elevated and curled abdomen of a nymph that has been knocked into the current. This is the kind of observation that's made by someone who does nearly as much seeing as he does looking.

If you get very serious about fly-fishing, you'll sooner or later start thinking about tying your own flies. You think it could save you some money. It seems like a neat thing to do: making imitations of insects out of fur, feathers, and thread through a process that seems, before you sit down to try it, almost alchemical. Finally you begin to see it as an integral part of the sport and it becomes a challenge.

You might argue with yourself a little:

"I *should* do this because I *want* to—if I don't, it's because I'm a wuss."

"Yeah," you tell yourself, "but it looks really hard."

"What's 'a matter," you answer, "you scared you can't handle it?"

And so on and so forth until you find yourself down at the fly shop buying tools and materials. At least that's how it worked for me.

I began to rethink the money-saving business as the cash register rolled up dangerously close to three figures (it will probably go past three figures these days) but I was committed. As it turned out, it did save me money, but by the time that happened I didn't care anymore. I was having too much fun.

In the beginning I made all the regulation mistakes. For instance, I didn't take lessons, but tried to learn from a book. I remember sitting down to tie my first dry fly. I opened the book and it said, "Step 1—tie in tail."

"Fine," I thought, "but I don't know *how* to tie in the tail. That's what I bought the damned book for in the first place."

There are plenty of good fly tying books and manuals in print now, and the authors of some of them even make the logical assumption that you don't know anything at all about it. Still, most books will leave you dangling somewhere along the line by not fully explaining something that should be obvious, but isn't. It probably comes with the territory. Any book that described every minute operation in complete detail, down to the pressure of the fingers on the material and the tension of the thread, would be too ponderous to read.

If I had one piece of advice to offer the beginning flytier, it would be, learn the basics from a living, breathing instructor. After that, buy all the books you can find. They're great, and you'll learn a lot from them, just don't try to start there.

It took me a long time to learn how to tie flies, but I think I can now fairly say that I can do it. In fact, I've even reached that point where it doesn't seem like a big deal at all. Just the other night I blithely told my friend, Mike Price, that it wasn't hard. He didn't buy it any more than I did when I was just starting. I guess this is just the bullshit that people who can do something perpetrate on those who can't yet.

Mike and I are even, though, because it wasn't long ago that he told me hitting clay pigeons with a shotgun wasn't all that hard. Right.

It *is* hard at first, getting those little bitty pieces of fur and feather onto that little bitty hook. You feel big and dumb and clumsy, and the fact that lots of other people can do it is no consolation. Even the nomenclature seems purposefully confusing. For instance, a March Brown isn't really brown, nor is a Red Quill exactly red, although a Green Drake *is* green—sort of.

I bumbled along for several seasons, stepping at least twice into every pitfall imaginable, but stayed with it and eventually learned how to tie flies. I even did it professionally for a while, a valuable experience that taught me many good lessons, not the least of which was that I didn't want to be a professional flytier.

I also learned that flies are not tied singly, but by the dozen; that good quality materials are almost as important as skill; that a size 20 fly is the same as a size 10, only smaller; and a dozen other things that every competent amateur knows. Gradually, my flies started looking as good as most of the ones you buy. I don't consider myself an expert flytier so much as one of those guys who's been at it so long now he'd have to be a blithering idiot not to have learned something.

In time, you develop your own ideas about how flies should look, adopt the ideas of others, or probably do a little of both. At some point a personal style develops. Your ideas about fly tying, fish catching, insects, and any number of other considerations dovetail into a personal signature.

Sometimes it isn't that complicated. I, for instance, just try to make my standard dry flies look as much like A.K.'s as possible.

In any case, your flies become distinctive and, most importantly, they're that way on purpose. If you like them, they stay together, and they catch fish, you have arrived. I don't care what anybody says. A "perfect" fly is one that's exactly the way you want it to be, for whatever reasons.

Up to a point, most of us tie flies that already exist, if for no other reason than that there are so many of them. Still, fly tying is the kind of craft that invites, even begs for, invention. If you follow it even casually, you see the new patterns appear in a steady stream in books and magazine articles. John Gardner once said that writers don't start out with anything special to say, but they want to say *something*, and I think flytiers are like that, too. You see the few great ideas come along—Vince Marinaro's Thorax dry fly, the Swisher/Richards No-hackle, the Iwamasa Dun—and you want to get in there yourself. I mean, these guys are all flytiers, just like you.

I don't remember the exact day I went to my vise with the intention of inventing a fly pattern, but I recall how it went. I thought, "I can tie pretty good flies and those guys just can't be all that much smarter than I am. Right?" At two in the morning I pushed away from the desk thinking, "Okay, they're smarter."

I came to see that wanting to invent something wasn't enough. There had to be an idea, a need to fill, a problem to solve. Otherwise, you're just blowing smoke, and you create ridiculous monstrosities that won't catch fish or soothe your pride, either.

This urge to turn the craft into an art runs deep among flytiers, so deep that *Fly Tyer* magazine has so far filled twenty-eight quarterly issues with mostly new patterns and is still going strong. One criticism you'll occasionally hear of this publication is that some of the flies appearing in it are, as a wholesaler of fly tying materials once suggested, one-of-a-kind patterns tied for no other reason than to appear on the cover; flies that are never actually fished and that are little more than the products of fevered minds.

I think that might be true in a few cases, but if it is, so what? I mean, what's wrong with a fevered mind? I've had one for years and have had a lot of fun with it.

Even the most outrageous patterns in *Fly Tyer* have probably accounted for a few fish, but that's not the point. The point is, they're experiments, and even experiments that don't produce the desired effect are useful. If nothing else, they may simply illustrate the fact that a nymph pattern using a dozen materials, fifteen tying steps, requiring the bending of the hook shank in two places, and taking half an hour to complete will never be a viable fly. Then again, there may be an innovative feature or two on that fly that could be used on yet another creation—hopefully a simpler one. In these pages you see evidence of craftsmen taking things as far as they'll go. This stuff is actually happening out there, and I'm glad someone is taking the trouble to get it all down.

The folks at the magazine have recently published the *Fly Tyer Pattern Bible*, a compilation of 672 dressings for flies for trout, steelhead, Atlantic salmon, bass, saltwater, and (my favorite category) miscellaneous. This thing catalogs more brooding human thought than a five-pound Russian novel and is some of the most fascinating reading in the field.

New fly patterns come from a number of different directions. Some are designed to solve specific problems, like the propensity of some trout to become selective to a certain stage of a trout stream insect. It's this that caused the upsurge in floating nymph, emerger, and ruptured dun mayfly patterns in recent years. Sometimes it's the problem (the problem is invariably fish that won't bite) coupled with a new vision, which gives you the Iwamasa Dun or the No-hackle. Sometimes it's an observation of insect behavior (the LaFontane Dancing Caddis) or a reaction not so much to the fish themselves as to the character of the water, as in the Henry's Fork Hopper.

Nine times out of ten, it's some combination of all of the above, coupled with a deep ego involvement.

In some cases the genesis of an idea comes from the pure lusciousness of the materials themselves and the fact that almost anything can be wrapped on, or lashed to, a hook.

John Betts of Denver has become famous—or notorious—for his use of synthetic materials for trout flies, and this in a discipline that continues to be dominated by the traditional fur and feather types. Betts is one of those tiers whose ideas seem, in large part, to be generated by the materials he uses. His flies are gorgeous, effective, and cheaper to tie than many of the standard patterns. If his ideas ever catch on, the raisers of dry fly hackle around the country could find themselves selling brown eggs at a dollar a dozen instead of grade 1 necks for fifty dollars apiece.

My own bias is toward natural materials, but I don't have a long, involved moral system to back that up and have, in fact, been known to tie and fish flies that were less than completely organic when that was what the fish were biting.

I guess it's just that the natural materials are so pretty, even by themselves, let alone tied, wound, twisted, and stood up into things that are supposed to look like bugs. To my eye, it's the materials straight off the bird or mammal in question that give trout flies that wild, natural look.

Whether or not the fish actually care about any of this is, naturally, an entirely different question.

Of course, "new" is an interesting concept in fly tying. Sometimes a new pattern involves what, in the grand scheme of things, is only the slightest variation from what's already there; the kind of thing that anyone but a fly-fisherman might not even notice. You can couple that with the fact that the sport is, at the very least, five centuries old, which means just about everything imaginable had already been tried before any of us were born.

There are some persistent patterns that seem to be reinvented by a new expert every ten years or so, simply because truly good ideas never die, and other patterns appear because even bad ideas can take on a life of their own. Once thought of, they must be tried. Once tried, they must be fished. If they work, the ego kicks in. It's your baby and you caught a *fish* on it. Wow! We've got to tell the world about this!

Most new patterns have a brief moment in print, after which they retire to a few streams where they've caught on. There they live quiet but productive lives away from the hustle of fame, making their modest contribution to the rich regional nature of the sport. A few come into fashion and stay there for a while, and a precious few go on to become widely accepted, like the Adams or the Elk Hair Caddis.

It seems to me that flies for trout have been getting steadily more realistic over the years, which makes sense. The more the trout in a given stream are fished for, especially if it's on a catch-and-release basis, the more careful they get about the flies they'll bite. On many of our best streams it seems to have become a game of trying to balance the subtlety of our fly tying with the growing subtlety of the trouts' perceptions.

There was a time when you could fish a standard Blue-winged Olive dry fly to the Baetis hatch on Colorado's South Platte River and take trout pretty predictably. But then a few years ago the Blue Quill, with its cleaner lines and more realistic segmentation, began to out-perform the old fly. At the moment, the Blue Quill is definitely coming in second to the Olive Dun Quill as tied by A.K. As it comes from his vise, it's the Blue Quill except that the body is tied from a striped light dun hackle stem that has been dyed a dusky olive. It's trim, segmented, and also the *right color.*

And so it goes. The trout continue to get smarter while most fishermen lag behind a bit.

The Olive Dun Quill is what amounts to the hot new fly on the Platte right now, and when I suggested to A.K. recently that it might be even more realistic if tied as a thorax or a No-hackle, he said, "Why? We're catching fish, ain't we?"

Well, yeah, I guess we are.

But then sometimes it goes the other way. The Henry's Fork is a Mecca for fishermen who use highly imitative patterns, and the trout there regularly see, and often refuse, some of the best fly patterns you'll find anywhere. Oddly enough, though, the last time I fished the Callibaetis hatch there, the fly that worked best was the one with the straight tail instead of the more accurate split one and the wings that *weren't* mottled like those of the naturals.

More to the point, I've seen people catch trout in the Henry's Fork on a #18 Royal Wulff, which doesn't look like anything. It's great, isn't it? If you want to stay interested for the rest of your life, take up something that can never quite be reduced to a science.

Bass bugging is probably the best example of that. Sure, there are some realistic bass bugs—frogs, mice, moths, baby snakes, and such—but the guys who tie the flies that seem to imitate animals from another dimension are the true surrealists of fly tying.

One of the neatest I've seen is the Schmuecker Bug. It has a tail and a pair of what look like wings made of calf tail, a large, round head (I suppose you'd call it a head; maybe it's the body) made of clipped deer hair, complete with eyeballs, and a funnel-shaped cup—also of deer hair—facing forward over the eye of the hook. It looks like a poisonous insect from another planet, but the bass, who must have minds like Salvador Dali, think it's just great.

Schmuecker is the name of the man who designed it, and it is also, coincidentally, the sound the bug makes when you twitch it across the still surface of a bass pond: a soft, slightly pornographic-sounding, "schmuecker, schmuecker, schmuecker." This is probably one of the great poetic accidents in the history of fly-fishing.

Of course, there's nothing in nature that looks or sounds like a Schmuecker Bug, but it catches fish because its inventor has a deep, probably instinctive, understanding of game fish psychology. He knows the fish will grab this thing when they see it, though he may not have any clear idea why. What's even more surprising is that a bass fisherman, upon first seeing a Schmuecker Bug, will say something like, "Jeeze, that's beautiful! That's really gonna get 'em."

If you ask him why it's gonna get 'em, he'll look at you blankly for a second and then say, "Well, just *look* at it."

That's called thinking like a fish, a quality that all anglers have to some degree and that the best flytiers develop to the level of mysticism.

Virtually all new patterns, however unique they look at first glance, draw heavily on the past. Some are what you'd have to call Frankenstein flies, made of parts stolen from the bodies of other patterns.

A.K.'s Hopper is like that. He says it has the body of a Joe's Hopper, minus the red tag ("I've never seen a grasshopper with a red ass," he says), the wing of a Letort Hopper, and a deer hair head clipped square in what we now think of as the Whitlock style.

Does A.K.'s square head predate the Whitlock Hopper?

I don't know.

Does it matter?

I don't know that, either.

It's a handsome and effective fly that's gained a lot of popularity here in northern Colorado in recent years. It's clearly a new pattern, but the first time you see one, it looks strangely familiar, something that isn't unusual with a good new fly.

It's an interesting process when existing parts rattle together into a new fly. There can even be a kind of logic to it, but you have to remember that it's more like poker than philosophy in that the idea isn't so much to convince your opponent as it is to fool him.

A.K. and I put one together like that on the Henry's Fork a few seasons ago. We were having trouble with a caddis hatch where the trout were feeding well, but were refusing our flies. We had gone through our standard Elk Hair patterns and then the Henryville and Lawson's Spent Partridge Caddis flies that are traditionally used on the river. We were taking the occasional trout, but we weren't *into them* like we should have been.

So, one afternoon in camp, we brewed a pot of industrial strength coffee and sat down at our respective fly tying travel kits to solve the problem. We started with a dubbed body, over which we placed the tent-shaped quill wing of the Henryville, ahead of which we placed the collar hackle clipped top and bottom of the Lawson pattern, naturally adjusting the colors to the bugs in question. We figured the answer might be the crisp wing silhouette of the Henryville combined with the low profile of the Lawson fly.

It worked. We caught trout and we were damned pleased with ourselves.

Later, at home, I refined the fly a little. This is usually how it works. You tie the first rough prototypes hurriedly, in a rush of anticipation and impatience, and fish them while the lacquer on the heads is still tacky. If they work and you think you actually have something, you then try to figure out how to tie it.

All I did was fiddle with the proportions a little, making the wing a bit longer than on the originals, and coming up with three color variations—yellowish tan, dun, and brown—to match local hatches. Somewhere in there I added a pair of striped hackle stem antennae, à la the Goddard Caddis, for a little extra touch of realism.

The new flies worked, which means that the antennae may or may not have helped, but at least they didn't hurt any.

We started calling this thing the Slow Water Caddis, but I see in the new Umpqua Feather Merchants catalog that Rene Harrop has just come out with a fly by that name. Okay, fine. We'll think of something else.

I've since come up with yet another low-profile caddis fly that stretches the original a little farther in the direction of realism. I'll call it the Spring Creek Caddis so as to get the name in print before anyone else jumps on it.

It seemed to me the one thing no one had done with a quill wing pattern was to make the wing go all the way to the head like it does on a real caddis fly. It was a simple idea—as the best ones usually are—and the fly that came from it is also pretty uncomplicated. It has a dubbed body with a sparse palmer hackle. Over that, tied in right at the head, is the tent wing. When you tie this on, it splays the hackle out to the sides. You then trim the hackle flat underneath, making the legs. The antennae are wood duck or bronze mallard flank fibers, depending on the color of the fly, and they curl lazily back over the wing.

It's a pretty, delicate, realistic-looking fly (if I do say so myself) that fills the need for an anatomically correct smooth-water caddis pattern. Most importantly, I like it, and that *is* important in light of the crucial confidence factor. All things being equal, you'll invariably catch more fish on a fly you have some real affection for than on one you don't care all that much about, simply because you want it to succeed. If you invented the thing yourself, well, you'll by God catch fish on it if it takes all night.

I've always been awestruck by the tiers who come up with new and effective patterns on a regular basis. I've been at this for quite a while now, and to date I've come up with one and a half dry caddis flies and two streamers that have solidified into named, working patterns. Sure, I've had plenty of ideas, but they all seemed to have already been done better by someone else.

So, creative juices flow at different rates. Mine flow slowly or, apparently, not at all for long periods of time.

My two streamers aren't so much new patterns as old ones modified to a different style of tying. They came about as the result of a long feud I'd been having with monofilament weed guards. I didn't like them. I didn't like the way they looked or the way they worked.

I mentioned that to a customer in the Western Angler one summer day and he replied, in the tone of voice you usually reserve for six-year-olds who can't get the top off the ketchup bottle, "Why don't you just tie them upside down?"

The light bulb that went on over my head was dim, no more than 40 watts. I'd heard of that, saltwater tiers had been doing it for years, but I didn't know how it worked. The customer—whose name I've forgotten, if I ever knew it in the first place—sat me down at the vise and ran me through it. It's fairly simple.

It seems that if you take a 3 or 4x long hook and tie in a bunch of stiff bucktail at the eye that angles back through the hook point, the natural buoyancy of the hair will counteract the weight of the hook bend, and the fly will swim upside down, or, rather, the *fly* will be right side up, but the *hook* will be upside down. You know what I mean.

With the hook bend riding up like that, the fly is virtually weedless and rockless. As if that weren't enough, the hair wing further protects the point from snags while leaving it readily available to hook a fish. Neat.

Did you ever tie a streamer with a long bucktail beard that wanted to swim on its side? That's the same principle in action.

The body can be anything you want it to be, weighted or not, as you like. The only stipulations are that you have nothing— or at least not much of anything—on the bottom of the fly to unbalance the buoyancy of the wing and that the wing itself be made of some stiff hair that goes through the hook point. Beyond that, you can do whatever seems right. You can even use feathers as long as you have a good, thick hair underwing to keep them from fouling in the hook. The hair itself won't foul in the hook because, if you think about it, it already is. What more can happen?

Elegantly simple and downright beautiful. If that man happens to be reading this, thanks, I owe you one.

The problem, of course, was to adjust existing patterns to this style. I spent the next several days at the shop working at it, and it wasn't easy because the boss kept hassling me about waiting on customers and other minor details.

It turned out that almost any standard bucktail streamer would work beautifully. All you had to do was turn the hook upside down in the vise and tie the fly. I learned the hard way that you can't absentmindedly smooth the wing back with your fingers because you'll hook your thumb. Other than that, it was painless.

Some flies would simply go on the hook upside down with no problems, while others had to be changed some, either because they just didn't work or because they were too ugly.

The flies I really wanted to make work this way were my two favorites: the Muddler Minnow and the Wooley Bugger. These two may be the best streamer patterns in the world. The Muddler—as well as various other sculpin-type flies—has the meaty chunkiness that fish often like, while the Wooley Bugger, with its palmer hackle and flowing marabou wing, has that indistinct, but still somehow definite evil, nasty, lively bugginess: not fish, not leech, not insect, but alive and tantalizing.

The Muddler became nothing more than a sculpin head of

spun and clipped deer hair ahead of a fairly thick bucktail wing. The body is wound pearlescent mylar tubing over lots of fuse wire for weight. I used to tie them with teddy bear eyeballs, but switched to the more realistic taxidermy eyes when Bill Black of Umpqua sent me some to try. If you're going to go to the trouble of gluing eyeballs on there, they might as well look real, right?

It's a goofy, goggle-eyed thing that, on the coattails of the finest fly tying tradition, looks real as hell until you try to decide what it looks *like*.

The Wooley Bugger got a body of furry foam—also over lots of weight—a palmered hackle, an underwing of bucktail, and an overwing of marabou with a few strands of pearlescent flashabou for a topping. Later I added black-on-yellow painted eyeballs because I've been getting *into* eyeballs lately. I don't know if they help or not, but I like them.

I tied both originally as bass flies, tending toward the larger sizes and using wide-gapped stinger hooks. They worked, by which I mean that they not only caught fish, but were also pretty much weedless. Well, okay, no fly is completely weedless, but these were weed *resistant*, which means I was losing one where before I'd have lost six.

To be honest, I wasn't all that surprised that they caught fish, largely because they were both so close to patterns that had been catching fish for many years.

Then I tied them in smaller sizes for panfish.

Then I tried the small ones on trout and they worked there, too.

I was downright proud of myself and started passing some flies around to friends. When I was first asked what they were called, I said, "Upside Down Weedless Rock Knockers." I still like that, but I've felt compelled to rethink it. After all, fly names should exhibit the literary sparseness and restraint that befit the high tone of the sport. The best names are brief, referring to the fly's prominent materials, its originator, or both, as in "Quill Gordon." After some thought, I settled on Bucktail Muddler and Weedless Wooley.

You could say the world already has too many fly patterns

and doesn't need to be cluttered up with any more. The same could be said for all kinds of other things, including outdoor writing. The editor of a fishing magazine once wrote to a writer saying, "We've been running the same old stories for too long, we need something unique, you know, new." The writer wrote back saying, "Well, let's see, trout, bass, pike, and panfish have all been discovered, the fish hook has been invented, I guess I can't help you."

On the other hand, it's not really advisable to simplify your fly selection down to the elusive "few basic patterns" you sometimes hear about. Even if you could settle on the correct pattern for every bug you'll ever see on the water, there will still be those times when the correct fly doesn't work and you'll need something else to try. Something different.

In other words, don't get too organized.

For years A.K. fished with pretty little feather-winged midge patterns, but lately he's developed new emerger and adult patterns with wings of some kind of opaque plastic that has a waffle pattern stamped into it. The emergers have trailing pupal shucks made of wood duck or mallard flank, depending on the color of the fly. They're attractive and they catch fish, but are they *better* than the previous patterns? Who knows? The point is they're something else to try.

If you fly-fish long enough, sooner or later someone will ask you, "If you could only fish with one fly, what would it be?" It's one of those cute questions designed to elicit a revealing answer. I was asked that again just the other day down at the Front Range Angler fly shop, and, after all these years, the right answer finally occurred to me.

"If I could only fish with one fly, I wouldn't fish."

I t's toward the end of May; shirtsleeve warm most days, but still cold—rather than "cool"—as night comes on. The cottonwoods, willows, and dogwoods are leafed out and some grasses are up, but it all looks new and almost edibly tender. The efficient, hard greens of summer are yet to come; it will happen imperceptibly, but one day there it will be. Great Blue herons fish in the shallows, and a few Canada geese are still on the nests, though most are now out on the ponds towing dirty yellow goslings behind them.

You've been fishing the warm water for a month now, having been skunked, or nearly so, the first few times out. But that's part of it. The spawning of the bass and panfish starts early. Well, not "early," really; exactly on time, in fact, but sooner in the year than you have ever been able to get used to.

It's a holdover from childhood, reinforced by outdoor photography and magazine stories. This kind of fishing is supposed to take place in hot weather, complete with mosquitos, but when you look at your slides of past seasons, you see your friends in jackets and wool hats standing among brown cattails catching bluegills.

The spawning bluegills are easy. They'll hit any wet fly, nymph, or streamer they can get their small mouths around. All you have to do is find them, and that's not too hard, either.

They spawn in the same spots season after season, and you've been fishing these ponds for many years.

The largemouth bass are on the beds at about the same time, and, although it's not quite like shooting fish in a barrel as some say, they can be found and they can be caught. There's some debate over the ethics of this. Some say spawning fish should be left alone ("How would *you* like it?"), but you have yet to make your mind up on that one. In a sense it does seem unfair, but then you've been told by warm-water fisheries managers that bass seldom spawn successfully here in Colorado because of the skittish, fitful spring weather. The water warms, but then a cold front comes in and it cools down again. Or it snows, or cold snow-melt water pours in, or something. A change of only a few degrees can, and often does, kill the eggs. Most Colorado bass fisheries are put-and-take in one way or another. The fish are residents of these ponds and plenty wild enough, but few were actually born here.

From a management point of view, it's okay, but usually after a few trips you begin to feel cheap taking them off the beds like that, even though you're releasing them. They fight sluggishly, seeming puzzled, or maybe even resigned, and they don't even hit from aggressiveness so much as from a kind of housecleaning instinct. You cast a fly onto the bed and the fish picks it up to move it out.

Among these bass are some of the biggest examples of the species you'll see all year, but once you've seen a few, it's enough. You return to the bluegills, who nail a fly harder in the spring than at any other time of year, taking them on the 2-weight rod so they can show off. Then you hunt up some pumpkinseeds for no other reason than that they're so pretty. Sometimes they're in with the bluegills, but you know of two places where they'll be off by themselves.

This is all near shore, including the bass, but then you climb into the float tube and go looking for the crappies spawning in deeper water. This is a bit more cerebral, since you're no longer sight-fishing to fish you can clearly see, but working deep, maybe even with a sink-tip line, in up to eight feet of water. The fly is a size 6 Weedless Wooley in bright yellow; a new pattern, but an old idea. "Crappies like yellow," everyone's granddad used to say, and all those grandpas were right. Maybe they were right about a lot of things, but that's the one that has stayed with you.

It's spring and everything is mating. Remember the lady biologist you met out here once who was busy studying the sex habits of the frogs? She explained how the males just jump on anything, trying one thing and then another until something submits. And then she gave you that look that seemed to say, "Just like you, right?"

But forget about sexual tension for the moment. As if there were some justice, the first fishing of the season is predictable and it's here. It's almost as if there were some reward for having come through the winter without wigging out. It was a long winter of working, tying flies and watching crooked and/or stupid politicians on television. At one point you caught yourself feeling sorry for anyone in government who made a practice of telling the truth because there's no good reason to believe him. You found yourself missing Jimmy Carter. Remember that interview?

"What are you going to do now, Mr. President?"

"I think I'm going to learn to be a really good fly-fisherman."

You understood that to be significantly different than just saying, "I'm going to go fishing."

Now, regardless of the placement of the equinox on the calendar, it has become summer. The fish have finished their reproductive business and have moved out of the shallows. They're hungry, and, as luck would have it, lots of things to eat have recently been born.

They'll lurk in the deeper water during the heat of the day, feeding casually as opportunities present themselves. They can be caught then, but it's a lazy, time-consuming kind of fishing. Not bad at all, you understand. In fact, there are days when you're genuinely up for it.

You settle in the belly boat under a wide-brimmed hat. Between the chapeau, full beard, and sunglasses, the only part of your face that's exposed to the sun is your nose, and this you slather with suntan lotion—the waterproof kind. With better than half of you beneath the water line, you'll stay pleasantly cool.

The selection of a streamer takes what would appear, to an observer, to be some thought, but "thought" isn't quite the right word. You gaze into the streamer box, which, because it's early in the season, is still nearly full of flies, looking for some sign. Bright colors with lots of wafting marabou and tinsel to catch the light? Or maybe a more sedate, more lifelike eel or bucktail bait fish pattern? How about the meaty, mechanical-looking weedless crawdad? Maybe the rubber worm copy tied with the six-inch strip of rabbit skin.

There have been days when the right fly seemed to crawl from the box into your hand saying, "I'm the one," and there were days when it was right, but this time none of them speak. Nothing you know—or suspect—about bass clicks with anything you know about fly tying, so you fall back on "bright day, bright fly." That's something else a lot of grandpas used to say.

You pick a big one because, well, because what the hell? The same reason you used when you chose a small one last time. What you're trying to do is tempt intuition into your corner, even though intuition seems to have stopped off for a few drinks today.

The leader tippet is 2x (6-pound test) just in case. The big bass are rare, but they're here—somewhere. You could reasonably go even heavier, perhaps, but even the 2x muffles the action of the fly. You used a streamer with lots of marabou so that the breathing of the materials might make up for the wire-stiff leader. This is only logic, but it might attract a real insight.

Much is made of logic in fly-fishing these days, especially when it comes to trout, but the bass-fisherman is still often faced with trying to decide whether his fish will eat a red and white thing as opposed to a bright yellow thing when there's no discernible reason why he should bite either.

During the course of fly selection you and your belly boat have drifted out from shore. The light from the blue sky is flat and shadowless, and the surface of the water shows not a single crease from any movement of the air. Still, you have somehow drifted ten feet and would, if you sat perfectly still in the belly boat, apparently end up on the far bank in an hour or so. The pace of fishing at midday is a little quicker than that, but not much.

The cast is made quartering off to the northwest, toward the deeper water. The weighted fly lands with an audible "blip," pulling the leader down with it as it sinks in the clear water. The monofilament leaves the top in jerks as a section of it hangs up on the surface film until the increasing angle of the descending fly pulls it under. You should have thought to rub it with mud while you were still close enough to shore to get a handful. Then again, what's the hurry?

You watch the leader, knowing that a bass will sometimes be taken with curiosity about a slowly sinking fly and hit it. Or maybe—more likely, in fact—a kittenish young panfish with a mouth too small to take the hook will give it a tug. The fruitless noodling of a baby bluegill can affect the leader in the same way as the mouthing of a five-pound bass. The times when you strike and miss, you assume it was the former, but you're never sure.

With the leader sunk almost to the tip of the floating fly line, you begin to paddle the flippers, very slowly. You'll troll down the deep slot at the laziest speed possible; just enough to keep the fly moving. The bottom here is no more than ten feet down, with the weed tops closer yet to the surface. You want the supposedly weedless streamer to go just into the vegetation where a little bait fish would hide. There are no natural contours to the bottom here, just what was left by the steamshovels that took the gravel out decades ago, but there's a kind of logic to that, too. You'll troll about 200 yards down the slot to the south, then back to the north, then take the arm pointing pretty much west, and then back to where you are now. If it takes less than an hour, you're going too fast.

With the sun high and the weather hot, the bass are sulking in the places that are the most comfortable for them. They're waiting for things to be more to their liking and are probably in something of a funk. You try to picture it in terms you can understand. Imagine yourself when you're like that. You will not respond positively to razzle-dazzle, but a needling suggestion— that could work.

Thinking "Slowly," you begin up the pond. There are geese and some coots in the water with you, seemingly unconcerned with your presence as long as you're at a safe distance. The heron was a different story; being one of the spookiest of birds, he heaved off on his great, long wings as soon as you came in sight. That's why waterfowl hunters use copies of them as confidence decoys. Supposedly ducks know that, too.

The original plan for today had been to meet two belly boating friends here at about five in the afternoon for a few hours of bass bugging. It had, however, been one of those late spring/early summer afternoons when warm weather was still a fresh and joyous thing tugging at your mammalian consciousness. The fishing gear had been assembled and loaded in the truck by lunchtime. That left four and a half hours before it would be time to leave. There was plenty of work to do, but with this virulent a case of pond fever, it would have taken you that long to get comfortable in the desk chair.

On the drive out to the ponds, threading the dirt county roads away from the foothills and out onto the flatlands, you decided it would be a good idea to be on the water at something less than the ideal time of day for fishing. Instead of just arriving at the right moment (and congratulating yourself on your exquisite sense of timing) you would be able to watch it evolve from the bright, siesta doldrums of midday to those hours just before and after sunset when the fish, as they say, "move." You tell yourself it will be both educational and spiritually uplifting, as all imaginative excuses for goofing off are.

A few hours after you first stepped into the water, you're back on shore using the belly boat as an easy chair. The chest waders are rolled down below your knees so you can air out a bit. Neoprene waders are great for belly boating—streamlined and comfortable—but you *can* get a little ripe in them. It's suppertime: a half-hour rest break, the high points of which are a sandwich, apple, candy bar, and several long, luxurious slugs of water from the canteen. A cup of coffee would hit the spot, but the truck, with the camp stove and coffee pot, is parked nearly a mile away.

That, in fact, is one of the things that makes this your favorite pond. Of all the odd little bodies of water here, this is the farthest one from where you have to leave the car. It's not unusual to be alone on it, at least during the week, which is considerably more than can be said for what are known as the "front ponds." It's nameless, but you and your friends have come to call it The Bass Pond so as to distinguish it from all the other bass ponds.

Speaking of bass, you managed to take three little ones and one about a foot long while trolling; more than you expected. Then you switched to a size 12 Hares Ear Soft Hackle and took some small bluegills. After that it was break time, so you'd be fresh when your friends arrived. They're due in a half-hour, which means they should have been here by now. Any second now they'll be coming over the rise through the tall grass with float tubes strapped to their backs.

Soon the pond will move into its evening program. The bass and the larger panfish will come out of the deep water to nose into the shallows. This they'll do to the music of the spheres—the turning of the planet that drops the sun, slants the light, cools the water, and brings the fish to the surface. The catching of the first fish of the day on a floating bug is an ordinary, predictable event that still has a certain cosmic significance.

Your friends arrive, talking and waving in anticipation. They can see you came early and have been fishing. They understand and approve of this, calling you a sneaky son of a bitch and accusing you of spooking the pond, before they ask how you did.

"Got a couple," you say in your best understated Gary Cooper drawl, avoiding their eyes so as to give the impression that it was actually more than "a couple," but you're too modest to brag. It's a standard working man's gambit that stops short of actually lying and always works.

Your friends hustle into waders and flippers and string up their fly rods as you casually clip the still wet, plastered streamer from your leader and hang it on the drying patch, threading it deeply into the sheepskin. The only disadvantage to barbless hooks is that they'll sometimes jiggle loose from things like drying patches and hatbands to vanish into that yawning void where lost flies go.

You tell yourself you'll put the streamer back in the box where it belongs as soon as it's completely dry—maybe in an hour or so—while noticing that the drying patch holds at least a dozen flies left over from last season.

From this collection you pick a little pencil popper. It's a size 6, store-bought job with a long, thin, cork body, feather tails, and long rubber legs. The back of it is painted in a kind of frog spot pattern with eyes. You had just about given up on bugs like this, figuring that the fish can't see what's on the top anyway; that it's just a bit of fanciness designed to catch fishermen. But then there was that study, the one that said the bug resting on the surface bent the surface film in toward it, refracting the light so that the fish would see the bottom of the bug as it actually was with the top lying in a sort of halo around it. It could be true, and the bugs *are* real pretty.

This is such a standard bug for you now that you finally broke down and ordered several dozen of them, in assorted fancy color schemes, from the factory where they're made in Ohio. They're hard to find out here in the West. It's considered a panfish bug, but that, it took you almost ten years to realize, is little more than a matter of nomenclature. Bass like them. In fact, they prefer them to the larger bugs so often that you've begun to change your ideas about fly-fishing for largemouths.

The smaller bug is more like what the fish would be eating on a day-to-day basis. We like to think of bass waiting with ominous, predatory composure for the opportunity to eat a muskrat, but they couldn't actually do that, could they? They have to eat what comes along, and this thing splits the difference between damsel-fly, dragonfly, grasshopper, moth, and baby frog.

Also, you have begun to think, eating these things involves less of a commitment—less of a *decision*—from the bass than attacking a bullfrog or duckling. The fish seem to take them more casually and sooner, too; after less teasing. The biggest bass you've seen caught in this state—about 8 pounds—was taken on a popper a size smaller than the one you've just tied on your leader. It wasn't taken by you, of course, but by a friend you loaned a fly to. Sure, it was your idea and your fly, but *he* caught the big fish. Remember, fairness is a human idea largely unknown in nature.

The three of you waddle down to the water and cast off into the pond in your tubes. It is still what most would call "daytime," but the shadows of the cottonwood grove where the owl lives are leaning into the pond, and, although the air hasn't cooled enough for you to wiggle into the sweater yet, it is about to cool, and that gives you the intellectual equivalent of a slight chill. The social chatter is over now. From here on out, the talk between you will be technical and, with any luck, congratulatory.

When the fleet was launched, you just happened to be in the middle, and your partners now naturally peel off to the left and right, leaving you headed for your favorite weed bed. It angles out from the cattail marsh along a spit of gravelly sand that drops off sharply to what passes here for deep water. The fish like this. They prowl from the dark water up into the cover of the weeds at this time of day without ever having to offend their nocturnal sensibilities.

Did you subconsciously jocky for this position when you started? Did your friends, just as unconsciously, allow you your spot? You'll never know. It just seemed to happen.

It's early yet; not quite dark enough, but the light is bouncing off the water now instead of slicing in and below your dangling butt; the evening has already begun. The fish are hungry, that is, they're *supposed* to be hungry now. Sometimes an evening goes by with no action. You don't know why this happens, although you have determined that it is not, as some say, the phase of the moon.

That determination was made somewhat scientifically, and you're proud of it. Last year you got your hands on a lunar chart, one of those that farmers use. In it you could look up any day of the year and find it to be, for instance, a good day to plant corn, a good day to "kill noxious growths," but a bad day for slaughtering hogs and for fishing.

If accurate, this information could have been invaluable. It could have made you the hottest bass fly-fisher in the county, especially since this down-home, *Farmers' Almanac* style of celestial mysticism is largely out of fashion now.

But how to test it? If you fished only on good days, you would surely prove the theory because you'd catch some fish. It would be the classic self-fulfilling prophecy. Even if you fished on what were supposed to be good, bad, and indifferent days, you could still unconsciously skew the results because, to be honest, you *wanted* to believe it.

What you came up with was this: you just fished as usual, that is, as often as possible, without looking up the days on the chart beforehand. You made a mark on your calendar for every expedition—A+ for a good day of fish catching, A− for a poor day, and a 0 for one that was so-so.

After six weeks of this came the day of revelation. You sat down with the calendar and the moon chart and found, lo and behold, no noticeable correlation. Conclusion: the music of the spheres is still probably real, but it's not a simple melody.

Having approached within casting distance of your weed bed, traveling backwards in the belly boat, you scissor the flippers to achieve a smart about-face and scan the water. It's calm and unbroken, which is okay; the fish won't really be charging around for a little while yet. You cast the bug to within inches of the weeds in front of you, and, before you have a chance to give it the first tantalizing twitch, it goes down in the kind of vigorous but dainty rise peculiar to bluegills. It's a good fish, about the size and shape of your hand, a keeper that puts slightly more than a laughable bend in the bass rod. Nice.

A further advantage of the small bugs is that the good-sized panfish can also take them. You are not one of those fishermen who feel they have to change gears in their emotional transmissions when they go from bluegills to bass. They're members of the same family living together in the same water. Bass will eat bluegills, but adult panfish will also eat newborn bass. One is nothing but a larger or smaller version of the other, and full grown examples of either are completely satisfactory.

With the bluegill released, you cast again, this time farther to the right. There are nearly always bass here, but they are not in predictable spots. There's no sunken stump, deadfall, or other textbook example of where the big one should be hiding. You don't really know how they behave down there below the weed tops, but, in order to give yourself a handle on it, you picture them cruising moodily, sometimes backing into the weeds to lurk. They are a nasty, aggressive fish with a seemingly uncharacteristic shy streak.

The way you move them to a floating bug is by needling. Sure, there are evenings when they'll nail a popper the way that bluegill just did, but those are usually the smaller ones. The big bass are, for reasons that are unclear, considerably more reticent.

It's not unlike playing with a house cat. You know the game, the one with the shoelace. The adolescent cat is easy; flip the lace out onto the floor and she jumps on it. This is so easy, in fact, that it's only fun for a few minutes. The adult cat is a little harder. The string itself isn't enough, it also has to act right. The most difficult is the old cat—the seven-pound, sixteen-year-old spayed calico. Her predatory instincts are intact, but she's seen it all, having killed and eaten, in her time, everything from grasshoppers to baby rabbits. Roll cast the shoelace to where she's sleeping and she will open one eye just wide enough to register her boredom with such a clumsy and obvious ruse.

In can take twenty minutes to get her to bat at the string, and during most of that time the shoelace should lie still on the floor, twitching and crawling just often enough to hold her interest. If you're not up for it, she can wait you out. If you get impatient and wiggle the thing hard right in her face, she'll get up and find a soft place to sleep where she won't be bothered by the likes of you.

Her psychology is as much like that of a big bass as any creature you're likely to meet, and she hits the string in the same way the bass hits the fly: without completely buying the idea that it's real.

The bug has landed on the water with a splat, and the last of the rings it started have dissipated. By tightening the line you're holding in your left hand, you give the fly the subtlest possible jerk—the spark of life.

Was that a slight bulge in the weeds just off to the left? Maybe. There's often no hint at all that a bass is approaching, but sometimes there's just a little bit of one. Without anything you could point to as a clear indication, the surface of the warm water can seem to vibrate before a strike; an effect a musician/fisherman friend once referred to as "basso profundo."

In times past, when the light and the angle were just right, you've seen bass creep to within inches of a floating bug and then hang there looking at it, apparently thinking it over. Admit it. With all the evidence to the contrary, you've come to believe that bass think. What else would they be doing at a time like that?

You've also learned that, as satisfying as it seems at the moment, twitching the bug is the wrong thing to do. At the worst, it will spook the fish and you'll never see him again. At best, it will set off a whole new line of speculation in his chilly little brain. If he's there at all, he'll bite the thing in his own good time. You can't rush him.

You wait for long minutes and nothing happens. Is a fish looking at the fly now or not? How are you supposed to know? You twitch the bug again—tentatively, cautiously—and yes, just the shadow of a wake seems to approach it now. Yes. Maybe. It might have been a ripple from the wind, but there *is* no wind; not a breath of it.

The sky is still blue, but it's darkening. The sun is no longer on the water anywhere on the pond. There's a liquid "whoosh" behind you as a pair of geese land, but you don't look.

No question about it, something is about to happen.

Ice-fishing isn't so much a sport as it is a way of positively dealing with unfortunate reality. I mean, you can wake up in the morning depressed because it will be months yet before you can fly-fish in real, liquid water, or you can leap out of bed thinking, "Oh boy! It's the *height* of ice-fishing season."

Or if not "Oh boy," then at least, "Okay."

I spent a good part of my youth in Minnesota, and up there ice-fishing was taken seriously, though not by me. In some quarters it was considered nothing more than an elaborate excuse for getting out of the house, but it was also an institution—as many of the classic excuses are—and there were those who waited anxiously for the lakes to freeze hard so they could haul out their shanties, or "ice houses," and spend day after bone chilling day cooped up in a thing not much bigger than an outhouse gazing into the hole.

As I recall, fish were caught on occasion.

I peeked into a few posh ice houses as a boy, but spent little time in them. What time I did spend was usually begged on the most horrible of days. "The boy here is gettin' pretty cold," Dad would say through white lips and clenched teeth. It could be handy to have a kid along.

The few shanties I fished from were wobbly, uninsulated, and cramped; little better than windbreaks. People whacked these things together using the inevitable pile of scrap lumber that accumulates behind the garage, and the most common boast was, "All it cost was three dollars for nails and hinges." Some were very ingenious, and no two were alike. If there was any luxury at all it was a small, smelly stove that produced more smoke than heat and that looked like it could blow at any second.

You could get attached to a shanty—a good one was a little like a summer cabin, only in reverse—but the rule was it had to remain expendable. Sometimes they'd fall apart and there wouldn't be enough left to rebuild. Now and then one would be left in a single spot for weeks and then be found to be irretrievably frozen into the ice. Most of these were abandoned with little more than a single glance back, and then, fishing the same lake in summer, you'd find them washed up on shore or floating like the ancient wrecks of wooden ships.

Sometimes we—Dad, one or two of his friends, and I—would brave the open air. If you've never spent a winter in Minnesota, that statement may not strike you with its full force. There was a story told about a Swedish farmer who had a spread over in the eastern part of the state. One year a new survey was made and it turned out that he didn't live in Minnesota at all; that he was, in fact, a resident of Wisconsin. When the farmer was told this he said, "Thank God, no more Minnesota winters."

It was cold out there; deep, chilling, deathly cold. Profoundly cold. It was so cold the only way you could accurately express the discomfort, even at a tender age, was with a heartfelt profanity. One of my early lessons in the social graces was that words and phrases learned out on the ice are best not repeated in front of your mother and/or sister and that, unfair as it seems, Dad gets in more trouble than you do when one slips out.

My recollections of those trips have now blended together into a single memory: there are the stuffy aromas of damp wool and pipe smoke and the almost sweet smell of frigid air. I know we were sometimes in villages of shanties with populations greater than some of the nearby towns, but what I remember is an arctic vastness, the ice and sky the same off-white with a line of snow-covered spruce and fir forming the horizon. It's a scene that could be painted with three brush strokes and two swipes with a sponge; very Chinese. Maybe you'd paint a human being or two, one in the posture of a man about to be shot by a firing squad, the other stomping feet numb as clubs, both dressed as Eskimos.

Somewhere in the margin of the picture, almost as an after-thought, the odd pike can be seen frozen in mid-wiggle next to the hole.

This is not the kind of excitement a young boy craves, but I did it anyway. I wanted to be out with the men; I didn't want to be a wimp. I was curious about whether being a grown man was going to be as much fun as I'd pictured it to be; something the jury is still out on. There were any number of reasons, none of which constituted what you'd call an absorption in the thing. Still, I learned how to ice-fish, and I remember it, or, I should say, it's coming back to me.

A few winters ago I took up ice-fishing again after a sabbatical of something like twenty-five years. I'm not sure why, I just did. Maybe it had something to do with nostalgia, or with the fact that I'd fished exclusively with a fly rod for so long I'd almost forgotten why it was better than other kinds of angling. This did, after all, happen in the winter, the season when you can come to suspect that you've lost track of something, though it may not be clear what.

The first order of business was to put together a pair of ice rods, which I did with the help of Mike Clark, a bamboo rodmaker who lives just up the road in Lyons. They were made from broken tip sections of old split cane fly rods—scraps, basically—but when the guides were wound on, the grips and reel seats were installed, and they were fitted with a pair of Dad's old Pflueger level-wind bait-casting reels, they looked okay. In fact, they looked downright classy. You don't see too many split cane ice rods.

The rest of the stuff was easy. Scratch any fly-fishing purist and you'll find sinkers, swivels, bobbers, bait hooks (though they'll probably be *English* bait hooks), as well as a five-gallon plastic bucket to carry it all in and double as a seat. I didn't have an auger

(I've since bought one), but I had a short rock bar and an old, dull axe, tools I remembered as being passable for making holes as long as the ice wasn't too thick.

Coincidentally, it was about then that a kindly bait company sent me a bottle of "Bio-formulated Fly Larvae"—otherwise known as pickled maggots—in the mail to field test. They looked fabulously disgusting, and the label pointed out, needlessly, I thought, that they were not for human consumption.

To back these up I bought some mealworms and a bottle of good old salmon eggs. Back in Minnesota, mealworms, or "grubs" as we called them, were tops for panfish like perch and bluegills, while live minnows, in a wide variety of sizes, were preferred for pike, walleyes, and lake trout. Tiny minnows were good for perch, too.

Here in Colorado the standard baits for trout are the venerable salmon egg (the one bottled in red sauce) and the common red worm. To be fair, there's also a school of thought that centers around garlic-flavored cheese, and there are even a few Southern transplants who use home-brewed stink bait. Yes, there are catfish in Colorado.

You know how it is when you're armed with new gear, even if it's modest; you have to get out and use it. I called A.K. and asked if I could interest him in a little ice-fishing. He was less than thrilled. This is Colorado, after all, where ice-fishing is practiced, but where it lacks the deeply rooted cultural enthusiasm it has in the North. During the long silence on the telephone, it occurred to me that ice-fishing out here is more exclusive and arcane than angling with the dry fly in trout streams.

An interesting twist.

A.K. was finally swayed by the possibility of fishing where, in his current state of mind, at least, that possibility had not existed before. There was also the faint promise of freshly caught, cold-water bluegills lightly breaded in cornmeal and fried in butter to a golden brown in the somewhat depressing month of January.

We went, three of us as it turned out, to a local panfish pond. We were all dyed-in-the-wool western fly-fishers, but had also all grown up in the Midwest and so knew, in an almost instinctive way, how to ice-fish. Or thought we did.

We'd all fished this pond from shore during many springs and summers but didn't know much about the shape of its bottom. We'd covered the margin of it wading and casting, and that was all we ever needed to do. It was odd to be there in the winter. In summer it's a seething, wet, warm, buggy, muddy pond that's lousy with fish, fowl, and muskrats. We'd all seen it frozen from a distance, but to be standing on it was disorienting.

So we did what any rank amateur would do: we hiked to the exact geographic center of the pond, poked a hole in the ice with our primitive tools, and looked in. We could see the weedy bottom clearly, and no wonder; it was only a foot below the surface. So much for the innocent belief that ponds are always deepest in the middle. We were all a little embarrassed.

Then we spent the obligatory few minutes gazing around. This is typical behavior for the momentarily stumped sportsman. It's seldom clear exactly what we're looking for, but we've all learned that authoritative mountain-man squint.

Finally one of us remembered that this was a man-made pond—a little reservoir—and that there was a dike along the east end. The water is deepest at the dam, right? Walking in that direction we came upon some frozen-over holes.

Fishing someplace for no other reason than that others have fished there before may also seem a little naive, but in ice-fishing it's the accepted practice. Scattered single holes indicate test drillings, while clusters of holes in a relatively small area suggest productivity.

You're right, it's nowhere near as sublime as deciding whether to fish the dun or the emerger by evaluating the rise forms of trout during a mayfly hatch.

We reopened one of the holes with the rock bar and peered in. At first it looked beautifully black and bottomless, but as our eyes got used to the dim, filtered light we could just make out the faint tops of weeds way down there. This was not known as a deep pond, so we figured this was it, you know, *the* hole where all the fish in the lake were milling around just waiting for someone to lower a pickled maggot to them.

With two other holes open, we got to it. I rigged up for panfish as I'd been taught as a boy, with a small pear sinker on the end of the line and three baited dropper hooks above it at about 12-inch increments, all on 4-pound monofilament. The rig is lowered until the line goes slack, then it's tightened a few turns so the sinker sits on the bottom with the bait suspended above it. This keeps the hooks up from the bottom and gives you nothing but light line between rod tip and bait, making the gentle takes easier to detect. This is how some fly-fishermen rig gangs of nymphs for deep currents, and for the same reasons, too.

I used a maggot, a grub, and a piece of borrowed worm: a smorgasbord no panfish could resist.

We sat on our upturned buckets then and settled into a mood of supreme confidence, even to the point of exchanging recipes for bluegill. Breaded and fried in butter is excellent. Deep-fried with beer batter is good, too, with parsley and lemon juice. In every catch-and-release fisherman's past there is an old, black frying pan.

Being fly-fishers, we had the common misconception about bait. We figured it was so easy it probably wasn't even fair.

Half an hour later I, for one, was beginning to wonder about that. We hadn't caught any fish, we hadn't had any strikes, and had all, one after the other, begun to jig our baits hoping to attract some attention. I'll spare you the rest of the details. A fishless afternoon of fly casting can still be described in paragraphs of florid prose, but ice-fishing . . . . It's enough to say we went home without fish, and after making a lot of holes, too. If we'd have been chopping wood instead of ice, we'd have all had a cord split and stacked. I guess the exercise did keep us warm, though.

It was only a week or so later that Mike Clark showed up with the big fish. I was working the evening shift at one of those gas, worms, cold beer, groceries, and deli-counter joints just north of town. By "working" I mean I was waiting out a slow night with a cup of coffee and a magazine article about fly-fishing, something like, "Hot Tips for Spring Trout."

I knew what Mike was up to even before he said anything.

He came through the door with that look in his eye and his face was still pink from the cold.

"You got a scale here?" he asked.

I called over to the deli counter, "Fred, okay if we weigh a fish on your scale?"

Fred is not a fisherman, but he's a nice guy anyway, and how much trouble could weighing a fish be?

"Uh, sure," he said, somewhat uncertainly.

It only took Mike a few seconds to go out to the truck and come back cradling what, for these parts, was an enormous lake trout. It was a bit more than Fred had pictured, being, as it was, quite slimy, very big, and very dead. He kept his word, though he did look a little horrified.

The digital read-out fluttered for a few seconds, finally settling at 29.6 pounds—30 pounds to any fisherman worthy of the name. There was an appropriate moment of silence.

Mike was too jubilant to hang around and talk much, but I learned the fish had been caught through the ice on a live minnow at (deleted) Reservoir, and I got a look at the rod that was used. It was one Mike had designed and built for taking big fish through the ice, and it looked something like a trolling rod/crossbow hybrid. The shaft was short and stout, made, I believe, from the butt section of a pretty hefty spinning rod blank. It was fitted with a standard reel seat and a level-wind reel loaded with heavy line. The grip was nearly as long as the rod itself and looked like a shaved-down version of a rifle stock. Mike demonstrated how one holds the rod in the left hand, reels with the right, and throws a leg over the stock for leverage. He strained convincingly against an imaginary 29.6-pound lake trout.

Mike is serious about ice-fishing and is very good at it. He also likes it a lot better than I do. We've discussed this.

"It *is* fishing," he says.

"Just *barely*," I say.

And then Mike was gone without so much as a free cup of coffee and Fred was staring dolefully at his scale. I realized it was up to me to mop up the fish goo.

The experts say you need a minimum of four inches of good, hard ice to support a person, but they don't tell you how to determine that before you're already out there. On an empty lake, the accepted method is for one man to walk out a few feet and jump up and down while the rest of the delegation watches from the shore. Ideally, he should bore a test hole, but he seldom does.

I'm nervous about being the first one on the ice and usually *do* make a hole. On lakes where there are already twenty people out there fishing—and no one is running toward me asking if I have a rope—I feel fairly safe.

The ice can be squirrely around here, at the lower elevations at least, because the weather changes so radically. It can get rotten: slushy on top and corny on the bottom. The four-inch rule is for *good ice*. In places where it gets cold and stays that way, you can probably relax through the dead of winter.

In my humble estimation, it is never, ever, safe to drive a car on a frozen lake, although some people do it. This was a common practice in Minnesota, even though they lost a few vehicles, sometimes complete with driver and passengers, every winter. Do you have any idea what a car weighs?

I remember a newspaper drama from years ago involving a pair of ice-fishers on one of the Great Lakes. Superior, I think. They'd gone far out on the ice, towing the shanty behind the car, and had found the spot where the lake trout were biting. Fine, but when they went to leave with dark coming on, they opened the door to the ice house to find that the berg they were on had broken loose and had drifted out into the lake, out of sight of land.

They were eventually found and winched up into hovering helicopters. Passing ore boats reported sightings of the car and ice house a few times before they vanished forever in the spring.

A local poacher told me another one:

Seems there's a reservoir with lake trout in it where ice-fishing is strictly prohibited. "No Ice-Fishing," the signs say, "Ice Unsafe!" But it's up in the mountains and this guy figured it *was* safe after a three-week cold snap in February. So, he snuck in, snuck out on the ice, and augered his hole, only to find that the ice he was standing on was suspended perilously fifteen feet above the water.

"What did you do?" I asked.

"I tiptoed back to shore," he said. "Left all my stuff out there, rod, tackle box, auger, and sled."

The problem is, they sometimes release water from this reservoir in the winter. At times the ice falls with the water level and at times it stays domed above the surface for a while. Either way, it's madness to go out on it.

If the man had died it would have been his own fault, but the people in charge of making signs might have gotten better cooperation if they'd used a few more words to explain *why* the ice was unsafe. There are people out there who regularly disobey rules they can't see any good reason for, and with all the arbitrary crap going on in the world, you can hardly blame them.

The signs on American subways say, "Do Not Block Doors," while I'm told the same signs in England read, "If Doors are Blocked, Train Will Not Operate." That's a big difference. It treats the people a little less like cattle, don't you think?

A few days after Mike showed up with the big lake trout (which had got me to thinking, as big fish will do) my friend Jerry called. It seems the trout were biting through the ice at a private lake he had access to. I told him I just happened to be free that very afternoon and, with a little bit of arranging, I was.

It was midafternoon on a bright, cold day when we joined a small group of ice-fishers who were camped over *the spot*. We made a show of going to cut our holes off to the side, but, as we'd expected, we were waved over. It was, they said, a pretty small spot. We exchanged pleasantries as we rigged up. The fishing had been slow, and it would have been better if we'd been there yesterday. We also learned that below this congregation of holes in the ice there hung some salmon eggs, preserved minnows, worms, cheese, and, with our arrival, the deadly pickled maggots.

"Prob'ly work as good as anything," one man said.

In the group was a little kid. Since I don't have any myself, I don't judge kids' ages well, but he was not much more than three feet high, and he was dressed in as many clothes as his mother could get on him. His coat and pants were bright red so that, presumably, he'd be easy to find if he wandered off. He hadn't wandered off, though. He was sitting there stoically, holding his short rod, waiting for the promised fun to begin. It had apparently been awhile.

"You cold?" one of the men asked.

The little guy shook his head slowly, and you could almost hear him thinking, "Not cold, bored."

The older gentleman in the bunch surveyed my fancy ice rod and seemed unimpressed.

"That reel ever freeze up on you?" he asked.

"No," I said, though it occurred to me it might if I ever got the line wet.

His rig—a tip section from an old glass spinning rod stuck into a wooden dowel with pegs to hold a few turns of extra line—was more what I remembered from the old days. Cheap, simple, no moving parts. Off the tip of this rod there stuck a two-inch length of piano wire with a V-shaped bend in it that held the line. On the end of the wire was a brass bead for a strike indicator. I remembered that, too. Any little bobble in the line is telegraphed to that piece of fine wire. The rod was propped on a wooden stand with the tip only inches from the water so that any jiggles would be from a fish and not the wind.

My own rod was propped flimsily on chunks of ice, and the hooks were suspended beneath a small bobber. I expected smashing strikes to my maggots.

Now I can only watch a bobber for so long. That, in fact, is one of the many reasons why I took up fly-fishing; you may not always be catching fish, but at least you're doing *something*. The day was cold, and I was beginning to feel it, even though I was packed in long johns, layers of wool, and a good parka. My feet were at least dry in rubber moon boots. When I spotted a bottle of brandy going around, I moseyed over casually and more or less got in line, making the usual comments on the weather.

Strolling back in the general direction of my hole, I saw that my bobber was under the surface. I dashed the last few yards, fell down, skidded to a stop, and snatched up the rod—rather gracefully, I thought, all things considered. I set hard on nothing and heard someone say that a feller has to have an empty stomach and a wet ass before he can catch fish.

It turned out the bobber had shipped water and just sunk. That particular red and white job had come from Dad's old tackle box. Imagine, a five-cent bobber that only lasted twenty-five or thirty years. I felt cheated.

I went to a tight line then and watched the rod tip, remembering my father saying, "A fisherman *holds* his rod," in that tone of voice he had that gave the impression the words were written in faded ink in the family Bible.

We spent several more hours out there getting progressively colder. Jerry borrowed an auger and cut a hole farther out in the lake. He fished through it for a long time, looking lonely away from the small crowd. The wind came up, making the gritty snow crawl in a pretty, Siberian sort of way.

Did I mention it was getting colder?

The man who was by now obviously the kid's father checked on him often. He'd sat there like a sphinx for so long I was beginning to worry myself, but when a nice, foot-long rainbow was caught, he ran over to watch. He was allowed to give the fish a long, hands-on examination and was clearly fascinated. Then he rushed back to his rod and settled in with renewed concentration.

For that matter, so did we all.

That was the first of only three or four trout that came through the ice that day. The little guy didn't catch any and neither did I, but I don't think either of us considered giving up fishing because of it. Sometime during the afternoon my hooks were cleaned, though I never saw or felt a thing. It was as if my maggots had just dissolved in the cold water, which, now that I think about it, may be exactly what happened. All in all, it was what I remembered as a normal day of ice-fishing. We broke up as dusk came on, and the kid left as reluctantly as anyone.

I'm tempted to say I glimpsed my long lost childhood in that kid, turned over a new leaf, and solemnly rededicated myself to the contemplative art of ice-fishing, but those are the things we make up later to make life look as though it progresses with some kind of logic, which, of course, it doesn't. All that happened was,

I drove home thinking about fly-fishing, wondering when the lakes would thaw, when the rivers would clear. At the house I started a fire, fed the dog, put supper on, and began going through drawers and tool boxes looking for a piece of piano wire.

TRANSITIONS

The day started with trout rising sporadically to a sparse mix of dark-colored, size 22 midges and some residual Black & White mayfly spinners. The spinners were left over from the fall we'd have hit had we gotten out of bed two hours earlier. The air was still and pleasantly cool for a summer morning, and there was a high, thin, unmoving overcast that kept the sunlight off the water.

It was a Wednesday, possibly the best day of the week to fish. Even those who snuck weekend-extending sick days (fly-fishers get sick a lot at certain times of the year) have relented and gone back to work, hoping the boss doesn't notice the tan. The Friday-grabbing early weekenders are still a couple of days away. The concept of the "work week" is one of the more deadening aspects of our civilization, robbing us of, among other things, all the great ideas that could be hatched by people who'd do their best thinking at two in the morning if they weren't too tired from working all day, but it almost seems like a good idea on those days when you find yourself off the conveyor belt. There you are fishing while most of the people who would dearly love to be out there with you are stuck at the office.

Smugness isn't the kindest emotion you can have at a time like that, but it's hard to avoid.

We briefly discussed pulling out at 4:00 A.M. instead of 6:00 next time so as to hit the spinners, while A.K. tied on one of his pretty little winged midge patterns. He started hooking fish on it almost immediately, by which I mean he had one on before I had walked downstream to where I wanted to be.

But down there the fish didn't want the dry midge, even though mine was a pretty good copy of the one A.K. ties. That meant—on that hatch on that river—that they probably wanted the half-emerged adult, the one still trailing the nearly shed pupal husk behind it in the water.

I'll never understand what it is about trout and midges. The bugs are the smallest of fishable trout stream insects—they can look like nothing more than a scattering of wheat chaff on the water—but trout are often more picky about them than about anything else they eat. It's a burden we all have to bear.

I now carry some midge flies with tiny hackle points tied in at the back to copy that trailing shuck, but back then I solved the problem by cutting the wing back to half-length on a fly twice as long as the naturals. That works almost, but not quite, as well. It worked then. I hooked a trout and glanced upstream to make sure A.K. was looking.

There were none of the tiny mayfly spinners on the water where I was, and they may have vanished up where A.K. was fishing, too. There had only been a few of them; just enough to testify to the fishing we'd already missed.

The spinner fall was over and the midge hatch rose and fell. The trout switched exclusively to the fully hatched adults toward the end when there were few, if any, emergers left. Somewhere in there I switched to the adult pattern after too many casts with the emerger fly had gone unnoticed.

Exactly when most of the trout switched to the Blue-winged Olive mayflies I don't know, but *I* switched when the action on the adult midge pattern slowed and when A.K., who was playing what looked like a hell of a big fish upstream, called out to me four syllables I couldn't make out at that distance, but that had to be "Blue-winged Olive" judging by the river and the time of year.

I knew he'd hooked the fish on a dry fly because "Blue-winged Olive nymph" would have been five syllables, and "Blue-winged

Olive emerger" would have been seven. I also knew he'd make the distinction; that's one of the practical advantages of having a regular fishing partner. There was also a self-satisfied lilt to his voice, and the nymph would have called for a more purely informative tone. A.K. isn't quite a dry fly purist, but he has distinct tendencies in that direction.

And yes, now that he'd mentioned it, there *were* a few of the little mayfly duns on the water, but not many, and the rises had petered off to just a few here and there.

So I tied on a nymph, along with a few turns of lead on the leader to sink it, figuring that early in the hatch there would be more nymphs under the surface than dries on top, and so, naturally, that's where most of the fish would be feeding: down near the bottom. Maybe I'd even make a smooth transition, going boldly to the dry fly while the nymph was still working instead of making the almost obligatory twenty fruitless casts over rising fish that tell you it's time to stop and pay attention again.

That's what I did. I fished the weighted nymph rig as deeply as it would go and then tightened the line as it swung past me going downstream, letting the current lift the fly briskly from the bottom toward the surface. This is supposed to mimic the swimming action of the emerging nymphs during an active hatch, and it seems to work. Sometimes the natural action of the current against the leader moves the fly too quickly or too slowly, at which times you have to add some rod tip or line hand action. But this time it seemed about right. I landed two fish and missed a couple of strikes.

That's one problem with fishing downstream. When you cast *up*stream to a trout, he's probably facing away from you so that, when he takes the fly and you strike, you're pulling the hook *back into* his mouth. On the downstream drift, the fish is facing you and you're pulling the hook *out of* his mouth. That, I think, is a typical anglers' simplification—I've been told that the actual physiological mechanics of missed downstream strikes are a little more complicated than that. But that's what it *feels* like.

Then, with the nymph still drawing takes, but with more duns on the water and noticeably more rising trout, I switched to the dry fly and hooked a fish right off.

It felt great, like I knew exactly what I was doing. It felt so good, in fact, that I fished the dun right past the moment when most of the trout began ignoring the few mayflies that were left on the water in favor of an increasing number of emerging midges. So I got my twenty fruitless casts in anyway.

I reeled in and started looking around on the surface of the water to see if I could figure out what had changed. I've seen other fishermen do this often enough to know what it looks like from a distance: if you didn't know the guy was looking at bugs, you'd assume he'd just dropped something.

I fished the midge hatch more or less logically: first with a pupa on the bottom, then with the same fly up in the surface film, and finally with the winged dry as the hatch petered out. Logic outstripped reality toward the end there when the dry midge ceased to work because there was yet another midge on the water— this one bigger and darker—that had apparently been coming off for so long that the emerger didn't work nearly as well as the dry, which I finally, bumblingly, got around to trying.

And so on . . .

It went on like that for the better part of nine hours, with the usual little dead spot around midafternoon. I had fished in the quasi-scientific way I fall into during multiple hatches—heavy on popularized entomological theory, light on intuition—while A.K. had stayed pretty much with various dry flies the whole time. He can do that. He can go to the dry when there's only just the ghost of a chance and make it work. It's a skill that has to do with accurate casting, the ability to "time" a rising trout, and slightly superhuman persistence. Or maybe stubbornness.

As we walked out to the trailhead that evening, we guessed that we'd each released between a dozen and fifteen trout, including a few that took line from the reel and drooped heavily in the landing net. A.K. and I long ago agreed to pointedly lose count of the number of fish we catch at about three or four, to avoid the creeping nastiness of competition. This way it doesn't matter if he caught ten and I only caught eight; what matters is, we both got some. We settled at three or four because that's the point where it becomes obvious that you're actually *catching*—

as opposed to blundering into—fish.

It had been a fine day. Better than fine, actually. Even on a river as rich as the one we'd been fishing, that kind of sustained feeding activity is exceptional. We were pleasantly bushed physically, but emotionally exhausted and fairly glowing with victory and self-congratulation. It had been damned hard, but we had more or less stayed with it. This is the mix of feelings that, if you fish, you come to need as much as food or sleep.

It was late that night—on a lonely, dark county road, halfway through a fresh thermos of truck-stop coffee—that one of us observed, "There is never just *one thing* happening on a trout stream." Neither of us now remembers who said it, it just rattled out in the course of winding down and getting home, but it strikes me as a good motto. I'm thinking of having it embroidered on my fly vest.

It's not a new thought. It was probably Heraclitus of Ephesus, one of those ancient Greek philosophers, who first pointed out that the world is in such a state of constant change that one can never step into the same river twice. When I read that back in my college days, I couldn't help wondering if there was any good fishing in Ephesus (wherever that is) back around 400 B.C. The analogy had a faint angling ring to it. Some centuries later Roderick Haig-Brown said, "A river never sleeps." It's an unavoidable conclusion that's reached by anyone who looks long and hard at rivers; or, for that matter, trout lakes, bass ponds, and so on: there is never just one thing happening, at least not for long.

It's an observation that, like most, doesn't completely sink in until you arrive at it yourself, but once it happens you begin to look at rivers in a perceptibly different way. All of a sudden an emergence of insects isn't something that just starts and stops; it's a constantly varying process that dovetails into other constantly varying processes so neatly there are often no visible seams. To say that a Blue-winged Olive hatch stopped and a midge hatch started is little more than a linguistic convenience that says more about what *you* were doing than about what was actually happening.

Out there in the river, the majority of feeding fish were probably taking duns from the surface late in the hatch, while a few were still looking for the last emergers and maybe one or two were finding a few straggling nymphs down near the bottom. A small handful of fish—maybe big fish—were in the bankside eddies and backcurrents happily eating collected stillborn duns.

Meanwhile, back in the current, the midge hatch was gearing up. At some point, some of the bottom feeders started seeing more midge pupae than mayfly nymphs and switched to them, perhaps haltingly at first, feeding on both simultaneously for a few minutes.

Sometime later the same change happened at the surface, and there were suddenly more boils than true rises as most of the trout abandoned the search for the dwindling duns and turned to the emerging midges. Most, but not all. A few stayed with the duns to the last, finally seeming to settle for the midges because there was nothing else.

Somewhere along the bank, you could find a fat trout who was unaware of all this confusion and was quietly eating ants. And the one enormous boil you put your emerger over a dozen times but never saw again? Maybe it was a big trout eating a little trout.

Never just one thing happening. It's a pretty thought, but it's not *just* a pretty thought. There are ways to use it.

Some are basic, involving little more than a passing knowledge of the life cycles of the major trout stream insects and a bit of logic. If the mayfly duns are petering off and there are a few midges on the water that weren't there just a few minutes before, it's reasonable to fish the midge pupa on the bottom to pick up on what might be an ascending curve of feeding activity. You know the mayfly nymphs leave the bottom, swim to the surface, and hatch into duns, which then fly away. With the number of duns on the surface decreasing, you know there are very few nymphs in the water. The midge hatches in much the same way, so if the winged adults are just beginning to show up, it doesn't take a doctor of entomology to suspect that the water is full of emerging pupae. So, in a state of reasonable expectation, you switch flies.

It's reasonable, but not required. If you so choose, you can fish the mayfly hatch out to the last bug for no other reason than that you like mayflies. You can hunt up the last fish who's interested in that bug, maybe even searching out a backwater where the duns have collected so you can leave the dry fly on a little longer. That's the beauty of fly-fishing: you don't have to be logical if you don't want to be. That's why you can still buy a Royal Coachman.

Still, it's nice to be aware of what is, or might be, going on in the water. That way, if you leave the Blue-winged Olive on longer than bare efficiency dictates—or put it on sooner—it becomes an esthetic statement. That's how A.K. fishes, while I at least try to be a little more scientific on most days. Interestingly, neither of us outfishes the other on a regular basis.

These transitions where one thing subtly shades into another are among the most fascinating things about trout streams. Not only that, they're also hauntingly beautiful. Nonanglers sometimes look askance at the fly-fisher's delight in bugs, but they can be as stately as bighorn sheep or as cute as bunnies. Really.

Most of us stumble through transitions most of the time, feeling frantic and cheated because the fly that was just working a few minutes ago is not working anymore. For that matter, I'm convinced the trout stumble now and then, too, but once you come to realize that the only constant is change, you have a shot at keeping up with it instead of coming in late with the right answer, after every trout in the river has already figured it out.

It's the fine art of the educated hunch.

I believe there are certain fish that are pioneers in the field of transitions. These are the aggressive, hungry ones that switch from the duns to the midges first; those two or three trout in a stretch of water that begin to show a lazy boil when the others in the run are still rising crisply to the surface. You look at the water at your feet, see a few midges mixed in with the mayflies, and think, "Aha!"

It's a great moment, greater still when you're right and can make it work. That boiling trout takes your emerging midge pattern and runs downstream, spooking a dozen fish that are still taking the duns. It's one of the things we truly fish for: an occasion for self-congratulation.

Some of the easiest clues are the bugs themselves, but the rise forms of the trout are also helpful. If they're boiling and rolling, breaking the surface only with their backs or tails, they're probably eating emergers who haven't reached the top yet. Crisp, dimpling rises, often accompanied by bubbles, mean they're taking something from the surface or just a hair below it. Casual boils and dimpling rises mean the bugs in question are easy marks, drifting slowly with the current. Slashing, violent rises usually mean active bugs, like caddis flies, or maybe something that's big and juicy, like stoneflies or grasshoppers. If the water is littered with mayfly spinners, but the trout are charging around like piranhas, you're probably looking at a masking hatch, maybe the first darting pupae of a caddis emergence.

There are other hints. Remember the guy you talked to at the cafe that morning who mentioned the evening fall of Red Quill spinners? Maybe there are only a few of those little tan caddis flies buzzing around, but wasn't that the only bin that was empty down at the local tackle shop? You're way too late for the stone-fly hatch, but didn't a guide on this very river once tell you the fish here remember the big bugs and will hit the dry fly eagerly for weeks after the hatch is over? These things pop into your mind when your partner upstream—a good fisherman who has been taking trout all morning—is suddenly standing there with his rod under his arm looking into his fly box.

A time or two I've been able to anticipate the transitions, and one glorious time I actually did it twice in one evening. I was on the stretch of the St. Vrain that flows in front of the house— familiar water, in other words—working a late afternoon this-and-that hatch: a few fish coming up here and there to ants, beetles, the odd mayfly dun, maybe a cranefly now and then. I was getting some half-hearted takes on an Adams when I noticed a single Red Quill spinner bounce on the water in front of me. The spinner fall was what I'd been hoping for, and a long, careful squint up toward the riffle in the slanting light revealed a few sparkling wings in the air. The mating flight had just formed up, and the first fertilized females were just then dropping to the water to lay their eggs.

I gave it a few more minutes with an Adams, and then changed to a #14 Red Variant, a fair copy of the egg-laying spinner. The rises were still slow and lazy, not the splashy rise you associate with active, egg-laying mayflies, and I had only seen the one bug. Still, what the hell?

After three drifts through a current tongue near the tail of the riffle, I got a take: a vigorous, excited strike while all the other risers in the pool were staying calm.

I took a few more fish as the rises got splashy and showy and more and more of the big mayflies hopped and skittered on the surface, and then switched to the flush-floating, spent-wing spinner in an act of what I can only describe as bravado. "I'm as aware of what's about to happen as these trout are," I thought. "Maybe even more." As the fall progressed, more and more of the bugs would fall spent on the surface, and, since these would be easier targets, the fish would switch to them, abandoning their flashy rises for the more casual, energy-efficient dimple.

After almost enough casts to make me think I'd blown it, a 10-inch brown came up and sucked in my spent-wing fly in a classic casual spinner rise—the first one like it I'd seen.

It was fabulous. I caught myself giggling.

And then I reeled in and left. After all, I'd taken some fish and had nothing left to prove. If I'd gone on fishing I might even have botched something—the odds were in favor of it—and badly ruined the moment. Success in fishing is a delicate thing and shouldn't be pushed.

We humans love that afterglow feeling of just recently having performed at our best, and we sometimes take the opportunity to evaluate how we did it. It's rare for me to pull off something brilliant, either on or off the water, but it always seems to happen on the home stream where the pressure is all but nonexistent; where, if I screw up, it's a simple matter of walking back across the street and cracking a beer. On fabled rivers where enormous fish cavort, I can just about forget it. I seem to be at my best when it hardly matters.

Could this mean that ambition is not really the road to success? It's worth considering.

It may even be possible to *create* a transitional moment. One evening on the South Platte I was trying, without success, to hook a big trout that was rising to midges. He wouldn't take, and, as the hatch slowed down, he stopped rising altogether, leaving the last few bugs to his smaller colleagues.

I might have taken another fish or two, but I wanted the big one—you know how it is—so I cut my leader back and tied on a size 4 bucktail streamer. I figured the fish was a brown (and browns are notorious fish eaters), that he was still hungry, and that he was still over there against the far bank.

The big browns usually have a strong nocturnal streak in them, and it was getting dark. I figured he'd be out hunting little fish soon anyway, and thought I might be able to nudge him a bit. It worked. I was surprised and so was he. Browns don't usually jump like that when they feel the hook.

Not long after that a rather well-known fly-fishing expert said this could not be done, that one could not catch trout by fishing a streamer through a midge hatch. I counted myself lucky that I wasn't an expert and therefore didn't know that.

Sure, I *am* bragging, but why not? I mean, we all understand the nature of the subject, right? And, as I said, these things happen so seldom.

There may be an element of dumb luck involved in these things, too. The brown that took the variant before the egg-laying spinners were even on the water may have been the one stupid trout in the pool, the one who'd have taken anything up to and including a bluegill popper, though I prefer to think otherwise. The things that happen between anglers and fish are always open to interpretation. You can reinvent things without lying, and you can lie like hell while telling the truth—often without knowing it. Even the stories told by good-hearted fishermen are probably best thought of as creative nonfiction.

None of this amounts to a new and revolutionary way to catch trout. It's more like an interesting little wrinkle; another small challenge, if that word hasn't already been overused. Anticipating the transitions and fishing through them smoothly can give you a feeling for what it must be like to be a real master fly-fisher.

That's when it works. When it doesn't work it simply shows you that it does, in fact, take a little doing to pull off.

Will you catch more fish? I don't think so. Will they be bigger? Probably not. All that will happen is that in the course of a season, a few fish will stand out in your mind, not because they were huge or called for a beautifully long cast, but because they punctuated a moment when you came to understand something about trout streams. You remember things like that.

W hen I moved to Colorado, almost twenty years ago now, I had yet to catch a trout. In fact, the only ones I'd seen in the flesh were in restaurants, garnished with parsley and lemon slices, and there'd been damned few of those. They were 10 or 12 inches long, baked colorless, and they looked, to the eye of a midwestern warm-water fisherman, like muskie bait stuffed with crab meat. They tasted pretty good, though.

Still, like fishermen everywhere, I knew the mythology of the trout and the fly rod, and I was ripe for conversion. Within weeks of my arrival in the state, I had a brand-new, bright yellow, Wright & McGill fiberglass fly rod that cast a #7 line and broke down into four pieces.

The South Platte wasn't the first western river I ever fished—actually, it took me quite a while to get around to it because it was so famous and intimidating—but it was the first one that showed me what fly-fishing for trout at its best could be like.

Where I fished it first was where most people fished it then: near the little town of Deckers, which consists of an iron bridge, a restaurant, a bar, and a few cabins. You could walk into the bar wearing waders and no one would bat an eye. For that matter, you still can.

Physically, this river is everything a trout stream should be. It's set in a pine-forested canyon with reddish to sandy-colored soil and house-sized boulders strewn around. It looks raw and primitive, as if the last geologic upheaval had taken place just the day before. The stream itself is small, by western standards, and very wadable at most times of the year, but it's also big enough to have plenty of deep, mysterious places in it. The gradient in this section is steep enough for some fast water, but still gentle enough for pools and glides.

In other words, it's the perfect size and shape for a trout river.

It was full of trout back then, both browns and rainbows, and they came in the variety of sizes that suggests a healthy, self-sustaining stream. There were great big fish, cute little ones, and lots in between in the foot-long, or "keeper," range. I naturally landed more small ones than big ones at first, but the good-sized fish were numerous enough that even a duffer could get into one now and again, through sheer persistence if nothing else. Plenty of trout for everyone, I thought then.

The Platte is a rich stream, and the trout in it are well fed and richly colored. The browns are among the prettiest I've seen, with bright, yellowish-gold sides, heavy spotting, and chunky bodies. And the rainbows . . . . Well, the rainbows have to be seen to be believed. They're a bright, darkish green overall with midnight black spots and wide, electric reddish to orange stripes down their sides. Many of them also have metallic-orange gill covers, and some even show the orange jaw slash of the cutthroat hybrid.

The South Platte *was* once a cutthroat stream, and turn-of-the-century newspaper stories tell of cutts in the 7- to 9-pound class being caught. Of course, those were only the fish big enough to make the papers, but they're evidence enough to sustain the legend through the style of extrapolation commonly used in journalism, politics, and fishing whereby the most extreme example becomes the norm. All welfare mothers drive Cadillacs; all Democrats are limp-wristed Commies; all the trout in the South Platte used to weigh 9 pounds. Still, it gives you an idea of what it must have been like, and it's a heritage the rainbows of today still show signs of.

The South Platte rises from tributaries in the South Park area of the state and flows down the Eastern Slope of the Rockies, through Denver, and out onto the plains. Upstream from civilization there's good fishing in much of it, but when most area fishermen say they're going to the South Platte, they mean the stretch downstream from Cheesman Dam, an antique structure that was built in 1906 and looks it.

This area is generally divided into three sections. The upper three miles is the Cheesman Canyon stretch, a fairly rugged walk-in that has been catch-and-release water for more than ten years.

Below that is the Wigwam Club, a section of very private water. I don't know anyone who's fished it (or who even knows who belongs to it), but presumably it's quite good. You know, the grass is always greener on the other side of the fence. And there *is* a fence, too; a rather formidable one. Research has shown that it is not possible to innocently wander onto the property.

From the lower boundary of the Wigwam Club downstream past the town of Deckers, the slightly larger settlement of Trumbull, and on to the Scraggy View Campground—a distance of about seven miles—is the 16-inch limit water. In typical anglers' shorthand, the upper section is known as "The Canyon" and the lower is usually referred to as "Deckers."

The Deckers stretch has always been popular at least in part because of its easy access. A two-lane road, with a couple of one-lane bridges on it, runs within sight of the river with plenty of places to turn off and park. It's one of those roads where vehicles often stray over the center line as both driver and passengers scan the water for rising trout. Sudden stops are also common. There's a little bit of private land along here, but you can still get on the river just about anywhere you want to.

Back when I began fishing it, there were no special regulations of any kind. The daily bag limit was eight fish—as it was throughout the state then—and you could use bait. Even with no restrictions, a large percentage of the fishermen were using fly rods, and some were even practicing that newfangled ethic of not keeping all the fish they were legally entitled to. Still, the proximity of the stream to Denver (in recent years they've started calling it an "urban fishery") and the sizeable bait-fishing, meat-hunting contingent resulted in a good deal of carnage. By 1976, when the catch-and-release regulations went on in the Canyon, I was in the slightly uncomfortable position of being a thirty-year-old who could tell you how much better the Deckers stretch had been in the old days.

Of course, those weren't really the old days; the old days were always before you were born, or at least before you moved here, and you can only hold forth on them with real authority from a wheelchair. I don't remember—and therefore doubt—the days when you could "take a stringer of 20-inch trout with no trouble at all," but then there are those who now wrinkle their foreheads at my stories, too, even though mine are a little more modest than that.

Like many area fly-fishers, I began to work the Canyon almost exclusively in the late seventies because the fish were bigger, the no-kill regulations (the only ones in the state at that time) were classy, and because the Deckers water was going steadily downhill with more, fatter fishermen and fewer, skinnier trout.

Even before the special regulations went into effect, the Canyon was known as a place where big, smart trout fed constantly on tiny insects. "Constantly" meant that it happened often and *could* happen any day of the year. That's because it's a tailwater stream, lying, as it does, under a bottom draw dam. The effect works something like this:

The densest water in a reservoir is that which is at about forty degrees. It sinks to the bottom and comes out of the dam into the river, keeping it at a more or less uniform and liveable (for trout) temperature through the winter. There's also a procedure by which a reservoir can act as a nutrient sink, making the water that flows out of the dam richer than it was when it entered the empoundment upstream.

High nutrient levels, plus a nearly year-around growing season in a stream with lots of good, deep holding water equals big trout.

Lots of big trout attract lots of fishermen, and that soon leads to a situation about which something must be done. By most accounts, it was Cheesman Canyon that led Colorado into modern fisheries management.

It also ushered many local fly-fishers into the arena of thoughtful hatch matching with light rods, fine leader tippets, and flies smaller than the ones you see for sale at the average hardware store. Moving from Deckers to the Canyon was the same kind of step up that fishing the Platte in the first place had been. It was the place where the big boys fished, and so, naturally, it attracted novices.

For some reason, I don't recall who I first hiked into the Canyon with, but I remember the day. It was late summer, the water was low and clear, and big trout were rising everywhere. I cast to them all day without so much as a concerned inspection of any of my flies from a single fish. I'd have been completely mortified if I hadn't finally hooked two smallish rainbows after dark on a #14 Adams. I remember thinking, "Thank God, at least *that* works."

I was back a week later with a spool of 7x tippet and a box of miniature flies and have been going back ever since, in spring, summer, fall, winter, and some of those fractional seasons that only farmers and fishermen perceive. It's not always hard, but when it is, it's like graduate school; the place you'd go to take a doctoral degree in fly-fishing. It's even been said that if you can catch trout consistently in the Canyon, you can catch them anywhere. My own experience has shown that to be less than completely true, but you get the idea.

The success of the Cheesman Canyon catch-and-release area in terms of angler enthusiasm wasn't lost on the Division of Wildlife, which began managing the state's best trout streams with a vengeance in the late seventies. That's another whole story that includes the establishment of Gold Medal and Wild Trout Water programs and the institution of special regulations across the state. I think it's fair to call it a success story.

In 1983 the Deckers stretch of the South Platte was designated Wild Trout Water, and a set of new regulations was applied: flies and lures only, catch and release on the rainbows, and a daily bag limit of two browns 16 inches or over. The rules reflected the fact that the rainbows were easier to catch than the browns and had, therefore, been overharvested in relation to the entire population. That's not uncommon and came as no surprise to the biologists. In fact, I once said in print that the Canyon contained rainbows almost exclusively with just a smattering of browns, and a D.O.W. fisheries guy called to say, no, it's just that the browns are that much harder to catch.

As expected, the river began to come back, but it took awhile for the fishermen to catch on. There was talk when the regulations began about how it "could" come back and about how it probably would, given time, but then, most of us had already written it off in favor of the Canyon.

Most, but not all. Rumors—those stories that pass for information in the fishing subculture—began to circulate. Good catches of trout within sight of the bridge at Deckers just like in the old days; a huge brown trout from a pool at an undisclosed location in the neighborhood of Trumbull; the fly-fisherman from Denver who had been fishing the lower stretch all year without saying anything about it—but who kept going back.

It's an interesting feature of fly-fishing psychology that allows us to ignore indisputable data assembled by fisheries biologists in favor of sneaking suspicions.

I started fishing it again after the word was out, but before it was *really* out, and yes, it had come back. Barry Nehring, a Division of Wildlife biologist who has been watching and studying the Platte for years, said that in the last days of the eight-fish limit it was rare to find a trout over a foot long in that stretch, which coincides with what we fishermen were saying. A normal 10-incher, he said, was at the end of its second summer, and there were precious few fish who grew to the age of three before being caught, whopped on the head, and eaten. "But now," he added, "there are lots of three-, four-, and five-year-old trout."

I was embarrassed. I should have known or, at least, I should have had faith. Instead, I let two years of good, relatively uncrowded fishing go by, only to finally show up after dozens of people I knew—not to mention hundreds of strangers—were already on to it. I shouldn't be too hard on myself, though, because the third and fourth guys who figured it out probably felt the same way.

On the other hand, a friend recently suggested that the smart thing to do when a new stretch of good fishing water opens up is to ignore it and go on fishing in the *old* spot. Everyone will flock to the new place, for a while at least, and you'll have a bit more solitude. This approach illustrates the workings of a fine, observant mind, and also assumes that fly-fishermen have about the same attention span as rock-and-roll groupies—a theory I can't bring myself to argue with.

Nehring said recent studies in the Deckers area show high densities of both rainbows and browns in the 12- to 18-inch class, as well as the usual occasional monster. People are still keeping fish—it's legal, after all—and this has resulted in a "stockpiling" of trout just below the legal size; that is, at just around 15 inches. He said that a few fishermen had been caught with creeled trout that had supposedly shrunk an inch or two since they were landed, but this is probably balanced by a significant number who return keepers.

There *is* a catch-and-release ethic in operation in Colorado, but it doesn't seem to have reached the level of cultural assimilation it has on trout streams in other places. It's legal to keep trout on the Henry's Fork, too (two under 12 inches and one over 20 where I fish it most) but I've never seen one killed and have only heard of two. In one case, the perpetrator was roundly and loudly booed by the assembled masses, and in the other there were some rude comments and disapproving lifting of eyebrows when a young teenaged boy came into Mike Lawson's fly shop with a freshly dispatched 24- (or was it 26?) inch rainbow. As the story goes, Mike, to his credit, said, "I'd have kept this fish when I was this kid's age, and so would all of you."

Last spring A.K. and I were fishing just upstream from the Deckers Bridge on the Platte, when I hooked a nice big rainbow. When it began to look like I would actually land the thing, A.K. waded over with his camera for the obligatory portrait of smiling fisherman with fat trout. A spin fisherman who had been casting from shore also wandered down to watch. When I released the fish, our audience of one let out a strangled "Eeep!" and said, "Jeeze, that was 16 inches, wasn't it?"

In 1986, the limit of two browns 16 inches or over was changed to two *trout* of the same length, and the catch-and-release rule on rainbows was dropped. According to Phil Goebel, a fisheries biologist at the Division's Denver office, this was done not to benefit the fishery, but as part of an effort to "consolidate and simplify the regulations," which the Division thought were getting too complicated.

In addition to the changes in the Deckers stretch, a two-fish limit, with no minimum size and no tackle restrictions, was placed on the piece of river beginning at the Scraggy View Campground and extending twelve miles downstream. This was done to avoid confusion and also, Goebel said, "To show people that the days of the eight-fish limit all over the state are at an end."

Catchable-sized rainbows are still being stocked below Scraggy View, and Nehring said the regulations there were "doing nothing except perhaps making the hatchery fish last a little longer." Remember that the idea in Wild Trout Water is to pretty much leave the fish where they are, while in stocked sections, the quicker they go from hatchery truck, to the water, and then to the creel the better.

I've heard stories about enormous browns being caught in the river below Scraggy View, but I've never been able to verify them or even get them firsthand. The trout in question was always caught by the brother-in-law of a friend of a friend of the teller of the tale. As one who has heard many a wild fish story from many a smiling local, I'm skeptical. Then again, stranger things have happened on trout streams.

The return of the Deckers fishery was a nice little secret for a season or two, but good news travels fast among fishermen. Nehring said that in the summer of 1986 the seven-mile Deckers stretch received an average of 10,000 fisherman hours per month, the highest ever recorded there. Catch rates have remained high—about 10,000 trout per month, or an average of one trout per hour per fisherman—and the regulations seem to be working. Fish sizes and numbers are up and surveys suggest that fishermen are keeping only about half of the legal 16-inch or longer trout that they land. Naturally, the results of any census of fish caught where the fish aren't actually there as proof are suspect. If fishermen will lie to each other, they'll certainly lie to a ranger. Still, you can get a rough idea of what's going on.

For all practical purposes, the river is back to its old self again, except that more people are fishing it than ever before.

Nehring agrees with local anglers that the fishing pressure at Deckers declines significantly in the fall when the weather turns cold and hunting seasons compete for the attention of sportsmen. Of course, there are few days in a whole year when you could plan on having the river all to yourself, and on the handful of days when you could, you wouldn't want it. Because of the tailwater effect from upstream, it stays fishable very late into the year and is one of the few places where a northern Colorado fly-fisher can take his Christmas trout and, in a mild winter, his New Year's trout, too.

Of course, the Cheesman Canyon water, which is closer to the dam, is the more reliable year-around fishery and is also an area that can be crowded on any day of the year. More and more people are fishing it in the winter to avoid the warm-weather crowds.

It was in February a few years back that A.K. and I had either our best or worst day in the Canyon, depending on whether you figure numbers of fish or discomfort as the measure.

It was supposed to have been a warm winter day, or so the weatherman had said, but in the mountains the weather isn't so much predicted as it is narrated. When we got to the trailhead, it was snowing lightly. By the time we reached the river, the air temperature was around thirty degrees, snow was slanting down at a fair angle to the ground, and there was a stiff wind chill in effect. There were also trout rising to Blue-winged Olives for as far as we could see in either direction. It was so cold that, rising trout or not, the first thing we did was gather wood and build a fire. That's cold.

The mayflies were slow to get off the water, and the trout were eager, but every time we got into a trout that took line that came back wet, it would freeze in the guides and, if it got that far, on the reel as well. Unhooking and releasing the fish would also numb the hands in a matter of seconds. So every trout landed meant a trip back to the fire to thaw fisherman and tackle. We kept the fire and the coffee going all afternoon and lost track of the number of trout we caught.

Everyone who fishes the Canyon in winter has his own "it was so cold my (whatever) froze" story. The punch line is always something like, "It was probably pretty stupid. One dunk in the river and I'd have been hypothermic in a matter of seconds." A.K. and I have agreed that we'll never do it again on purpose, but if we stumble into the same thing again by accident, I'd hate to be the one to suggest we turn around and go home.

That was the only day in going on two decades of fishing the Platte when I've seen the Canyon empty. People want to fish quality water, even when the fish catching is next to impossible and they have to suffer to do it. In fact, Nehring has said that this stretch of the South Platte, with its three special regulation areas laid end to end, illustrates a growing acceptance of this kind of fisheries management. "The more restrictive the regulations," he said, "the heavier the fishing pressure."

From a technical standpoint, the fishing in all three sections is roughly the same, except that the Canyon, where all the trout have lived their entire lives under no-kill rules, is the most difficult, and the stocked water is, by all accounts, the easiest. Most of the food organisms are small, with mayflies and midges predominating. Except in the highest flows, the fishing can be delicate and tricky.

The premier hatch is the Blue-winged Olive mayfly. It's a size 20 or 22—there are two insects involved, I'm told—and the best hatches tend to be in the fall, although there can be sporadic, unexpected emergences at other times of the year. As you'd suspect in heavily fished water, the trout are pretty selective at times, and fly pattern can be crucial.

There are other good mayfly hatches up and down the river, including Red Quills and the tiny White-winged Blacks, which produce fascinating falls of #22 or even #24 spinners on late summer mornings. There are other mayflies, some caddis, and midge hatches that seem almost constant. The fishing with standard dry flies—hackled or otherwise—can be wonderful, but more and more Platte regulars are backing these up with the floating nymph and emerger patterns that often make the difference.

The Platte is also a holy place for nymph fishermen who use the short-line technique some say was invented on this river. It involves a single nymph—usually small—on a leader weighted with split shot that is drifted through the deeper holes. It takes the eyes of a hawk and the concentration of a saint, but those who are good at it are deadly. In years past there was some debate over the ethics of this, and you could kill a slow hour or two by starting an argument over "fishing lead." Such discussions are increasingly rare, however.

The most popular nymphs are mayfly imitations like the Beatis nymph, Pheasant Tail, and the regionally famous RS-2 Emerger, although some holdouts still favor the venerable Hares Ear in sizes 18 and 20. Midge larvae and pupae patterns are also effective, especially in the colder, low-water months.

Shrimp patterns are also good, and this is a subject on which you can still get a good debate started. Olive Shrimp or "scud" flies are fairly standard on the river, but a real favorite is the Pink Shrimp, which is, in fact, anywhere from pink to yellowish-orange depending on whose vise it came from. There are two opinions on this fly. One is that it's an attractor, nothing more than a Glow Bug or egg pattern, and therefore not proper.

The other is somewhat more entomological. It says that when the shrimp molt, as they do periodically as they grow, their bodies are a sort of flesh-color for a while until the new shells harden. The trout eat a lot of them then, it's said, because the little crustaceans are easier to see, nice and juicy, and are also more likely to be knocked loose into the current as they struggle to crack out of the old shell.

For the record, I have no opinion, but I fish the fly.

As on all great and popular rivers, the morality that grows up is built upon the old weird fly-fishing tradition, but it also develops its own peculiar twists.

With the shrimp question still unresolved, stories have now begun to surface concerning the effectiveness of a thing called the

San Juan Worm. This fly, which originated on the river in New Mexico whose name it now bears, is a professional flytier's fantasy come true. It's nothing more than a length of chenille lashed to a large wet-fly hook to make a worm about an inch long. They come in red, pink, and orange, and Walley Allen, who wholesales Ultra Chenille, says the current favorite is the color he tastefully calls Earthworm Brown.

The fly was originally tied to copy the annelid worm found in the San Juan. It is not an attractive creature, but it is, nonetheless, a legitimate aquatic food organism. Some say the annelid lives in the Platte; others say no, but the fly mimics a crane fly larva; still others say it's nothing more than a candy store pattern and any trout who bites one should be ashamed of himself. I've tied some up (boy, are they easy) but I have yet to be able to make myself fish them. I think it's the word "worm" in the name.

Whatever the case, it represents a phenomenon common on many upscale, catch-and-release streams; the one where the tweed and cane types with the minute, anatomically correct flies are sometimes out-fished by a guy using a size 4 Something-or-other in hot pink. Those who aren't completely freaked out by this see it as part of the river's charm.

It would be satisfying to leave the story of the South Platte there; with a fine, though crowded, trout stream with lots of big fish that supports a brace of quiet, funky little towns, and a vital, if not always agreeable, society of fly-fishermen. Unfortunately, though, there's more to it.

The Denver Water Board wants to build a dam, called Two Forks, just below the confluence of the North Fork and the main branch of the South Platte. Depending on the size of the dam, it could flood 60 to 80 percent of the river below Cheesman Dam. At best, it would flood the river up to Scraggy View. At the worst, it could go all the way up to Cheesman Canyon.

At this writing, the dam remains in the proposal stage with a preliminary draft of an environmental impact statement (EIS) just out and the first moves in the long, maddening chess game of mitigation being made between the Water Board and the Division of Wildlife.

Steve Puttmann, environmental specialist with the Division, doesn't pull any punches on the subject. "As far as we're concerned," he says, "this is an environmental catastrophe." Puttmann is looking into the possibilities for mitigation on the proposal—the scam by which the Water Board would supposedly "replace" the lost resource.

Steve says that neither he nor the Division in general are willing to just assume the dam will be built (an assumption you'll hear voiced in some quarters) but that he's working under a "worst case scenario." Of the mitigation process itself, he says that if the dam *is* built, "the bill to the Water Board to replace the recreational resource will be immense." The only way they could even come close would be to "optimize the remainder of their system" by providing for the draining of all reservoirs to remove rough fish, guaranteeing minimum flows below all dams, instituting in-stream habitat improvements, repairing riparian habitat, revoking grazing rights, and so on and so forth.

The recreational value of the proposed reservoir itself does not impress Puttmann. "We're not prepared to trade our river value for flat water," he says, and he also feels moved to state the obvious: "The South Platte is the best trout stream in the state, and you can't 'replace' something like that. When it's gone, it's gone."

Just recently the Division purchased, at a cost of $1.6 million, 3,000 acres of real estate in South Park, the centerpiece of which is about six and one-half miles of the South Platte. This is upstream from Cheesman Dam and not in the disputed area, but it does seem to remove a significant stretch of excellent trout water from the mitigation process.

Was that intentional? I don't know. It's so hard to get straight answers in situations like this, and—although I hate to admit it—if there *is* a strategy in operation here, it might not be the wisest thing to spill it to a writer who will surely splash it all over a page somewhere and possibly blow the deal. Let me just say I sincerely hope that's what's going on, and leave it at that.

Mitigation, in case you've never looked at it closely, defies both logic and morality. Whatever is done to improve and enhance other fisheries, if they go ahead and flood up to nineteen miles of one of the West's best trout streams, there will be nineteen miles less. Is the Water Board going to arrange for a new canyon to be eroded from the mountains? Are they going to cause that much more snow to fall and see to it that a biomass evolves to feed the trout?

Even if they could, we don't have the time to wait. We'll be extinct by the time the next generation of trout streams comes along.

On the moral side, mitigation is something like what would happen if I, through my own negligence, killed one of your children. Even if I didn't go to jail, I'd have to pay you a stupendous amount of money—probably all the money I will ever make and more. It wouldn't replace the lost life, but it would be something, and your lawyer and my lawyer would be placed in the damnable position of having to hassle over what a life—maybe the life of the next president or the next messiah—was worth in terms of American dollars.

Mitigation is a step worse than that. It amounts to me coming to you and saying, "I plan to run over one of your children in about two years, what's it going to be worth to you?" and you are expected to come up with a reasonable figure. Through some voodoo, the decision to go ahead with the plan seems to have already been made. Your options have been mysteriously edited down to a list of figures, and while you're still saying, "Now wait a minute . . ." I'm already trying to bring your price down. "One hundred and nine million?" I say. "You've gotta be crazy. Let's look at these figures again."

If you had a favorite child, that's the one I'd want to run over. The draft statement just issued admits that Two Forks Dam would be the most environmentally damaging of all the proposed dams in the study, wiping out miles of prime trout stream, threatening endangered species of wildlife, and eliminating some of the most frequently visited national forest land in the state, but it would also be the most "cost-effective," which is assumed to be the ultimate bottom line.

Never mind that the population growth estimates involved

come from figures that were compiled five years ago when the growth rate was higher than it is now. Never mind that the draft EIS all but ignores the alternatives, including other, less damaging sites as well as conservation of existing resources.

There are those who will tell you it's altruistic; for the greater good; that we need the growth to prosper. I'm not an economist, as anyone will tell you, but it seems to me that if our survival system is based on eternal growth and expansion within a finite environment, then our entire culture is headed right for the shit hole. I mean, if we're going to suffer some from slow growth, what's going to happen to us when every last thing of value is gone forever? People are moving west largely because of our widely advertised quality of life. What's supposed to happen when the quality disappears?

As you'd expect, opposition to the dam is widespread in what is loosely called the environmental community, and the various conservation groups are even sitting down together from time to time to keep each other informed and otherwise try to get their ducks in a row. That's heartening, I think. Too often the hunters and the flower huggers won't even speak to each other, and the fishermen are seen by both as too weird and snobbish to deal with.

At the moment, the Water Board and their lawyers are trying for an end run. The recently introduced House Bill 1158 would have Colorado taxpayers footing the bill for all but a small percentage of the mitigation costs of Two Forks and other water projects, and would also remove the responsiblity for establishing mitigation costs from the Division of Wildlife and place it in the hands of the Colorado Water Conservation Board, the agency that *sponsors* water projects.

According to a legislative alert from Trout Unlimited, it would be a case of "the foxes guarding the chicken coop." Outdoor writer Bob Saile said it would be a case of the cat guarding the goldfish bowl.

You get the idea.

Sure, at this very moment letters are flying and fists are being pounded on tables, but by the time you read this at least some of it will be old news. That's not the point. The point is, you can't just be a slightly antisocial but largely harmless fisherman happily bopping around in the backwoods anymore. Now you have to come back from a pleasant day astream all relaxed and cleansed, sit down at the desk, get good and mad, and start writing letters.

That's the reality now. It hasn't ruined fishing, but it has sure changed it some.

A few months ago A.K. and I were fishing just upstream from the Deckers Bridge. It was somewhere between late fall and early winter, and we'd chosen that stretch not only for the fishing, but for its proximity to the bar. On cold days it's nice to take your break inside, on a stool next to the woodstove.

We'd caught some fish on midges as a low-pressure front slid up against the Eastern Slope and settled in, but then the fishing went off, and the next fishless hour had a feeling of finality to it.

With more daylight left than usual, we decided to take the long way back to the main highway, down the river to the ghost town of South Platte—nothing more than a spooky-looking old false-fronted hotel now—and then up through Foxton to the main road. A.K. admitted that he'd never even seen the lower stretch, the place where the bait-fishermen go, and I realized I hadn't seen it myself in a good ten years. In light of recent events, we decided we'd better go have a look at the place while it was still there.

It was beautiful. I'd actually forgotten, though once there I remembered well enough. A.K. was impressed. The road was poor, having changed from pavement to dirt somewhere downstream from Trumbull, and in places it was only one truck wide. That wasn't a problem, though. The water in the puddles in the road was clear; a sign of very light traffic.

The river itself is entirely recognizable down there with huge boulders and gravelly soil. In places it looks a lot like the Canyon, except lonelier. Even with the water down, some holes were tantalizingly deep and fishy-looking. I thought about the stories of monster browns and came a step closer to believing them.

We didn't fish, we just looked; something every fisherman should take the time to do now and then. Leave the rods in the car for once and just take it all in like a tourist.

In front of a pretty little cabin down there was a large, hand-painted sign that was, no doubt, in violation of some ordinance or other forbidding billboards in a national forest. Maybe they hadn't found it yet, or maybe it had been conveniently overlooked. The sign said, "If Two Forks is Built, All This Will Be Underwater."

W e all want to catch big fish. That's one of the things nonanglers have straight about us. And the bigger they are, the better we like them. The International Game Fish Association even keeps world records on fish in several categories—including fly rod tippet classes—so we can see how big they get and how big a one can be landed on various strengths of monofilament—presumably for the purposes of comparison. Big fish are old, smart, wily, and secretive, or at least that's how we picture them. They have strong medicine, and, in a satisfyingly primitive way, we feel we can steal their magic by catching them.

But what *is* a big fish?

You can't go by the all tackle world records because those are the largest fish ever caught by sporting means, and it's not wise to adopt a scale that will make your own efforts look paltry. Except for a few real hotshots, world records have little practical meaning.

State records are more useful. You're still looking at monsters, but at least they were caught around home and make some relative sense.

"Relative" is the operative word here, and fly-fishermen are highly adept relativists. In our hands the question ceases to be

"What is a big fish?" and becomes "Big compared to what?"

Judging from the stories of fishermen and the claims of guide services, any trout weighing in at 5 pounds is considered big in the overall scheme of things; big in the sense that if you are not impressed by such a fish, you risk being asked just who the hell you think you are anyway.

Using another form of measurement, any trout that's 20 inches from tail to jaw is big, even though he may not weigh 5 pounds. Some use inches, while others prefer pounds. The latter conveys more information. Some fly-fishers split the difference, measuring fish under 20 inches and weighing those above. That's because "18 inches" sounds better than "2½ pounds."

Based on the same stories and claims, a big largemouth bass (or a large bigmouth bass, if you like) will weigh closer to 8 pounds. To most of us who fish for both with a fly rod, a bass is a bigger fish than a trout, even though the world record largemouth at 22 pounds, 4 ounces is seriously outclassed by the world record brown at 35 pounds, 15 ounces and the world record rainbow at 42 pounds, 2 ounces.

For that matter, there are a lot of fly-fishers around who will tell you a brown is a bigger trout than a rainbow. But then, didn't I just say that world records weren't of much use in this context? Right, but how do you expect me to maneuver the discussion away from a 42-pound trout? After all, we're talking about big fish here.

What makes a bass a bigger fish than a trout is average size or, more properly, what is considered a keeper. This is a somewhat dated concept in circles where a keeper is now referred to as a "good fish," but it means the same thing: one you wouldn't be ashamed to bring home *if* you were to bring any home, which, of course, you're not going to do.

Around here a good trout is about a foot long. A good bass is more like 14 or 15 inches. If you wouldn't be happy to catch a dozen of either on a light fly rod, you are definitely out of my league.

"Big" is also a regional concept based on fisheries quality. On the Yellowstone River in Yellowstone Park, a 20-inch cutthroat is a big fish. A 20-inch rainbow from the Henry's Fork is also big, but, although it may be the biggest trout you take in a week's fishing, it's not the biggest one you can hope for.

Hope, as opposed to reasonable expectation, has a lot to do with it. An electro-shocking survey of a modest-sized brown trout creek might reveal the average fish to be 9 inches long, a few odd trout will push up to 15 or 16 inches, and the single old hen brown in the deep hole under the bridge weighs 9 pounds. Hope swims in the deep water in the Bridge Pool, feeding mostly at night. Some refuse to believe it's there. Among the believers are a few who think they've seen it. It's a fish that stands a good chance of dying of old age.

It's hard to argue with the idea that a big fish is the biggest one in the water you're fishing at the moment. In this context, a 14-inch brookie from a little beaver pond at 10,500 feet is the same size as a yard-long rainbow from the Madison River.

Late last summer I was fishing with A.K. and his old fishing buddy from Michigan, Bob Fairchild. We wanted to show Bob some huge Rocky Mountain rainbows, so we went and camped near a famous trout river. For several days, working in fairly crowded conditions, we caught fish that, in the context of this discussion, ranged from good to very good in a river where an 8-pound trout was once caught on a dry fly.

After a few days of this we took an afternoon off to get clear of the crowd. We drove up into the high country and hiked up a diminutive brook trout creek, a lonely little trickle that showed few signs of ever having been fished. It was up in there, a few miles from the truck, that A.K. landed a fat little 13-inch brookie that was clearly the biggest fish of the trip.

This relative-to-the-water-in-question concept gives rise to one of the most common sour-grapisms directed at famous big-fish anglers; you know, the guys with reputations as headhunters who are always pictured with enormous, ugly, dripping fish. "Sure," people say. "If I fished the places he did, I'd catch fish like that, too."

That's at least partly true. Most of us fish for the average fish. We go out during the day to cast poppers for bass, dry flies for trout, or whatever, looking to *catch some fish*. If we go to where the average fish are bigger than they are near home, well . . .

I'm as into this as anyone. I can stay home and fish the St. Vrain and the three forks and sometimes catch "big" 12- to 14-inch trout. No problem. Perfectly satisfactory. I use a light cane rod, tend toward dry flies, and have a fine time.

But then there are the relatively short trips to better Colorado rivers like the South Platte and Frying Pan. According to the last Division of Wildlife study I saw, the average trout in the Pan was 16 inches long, and there were plenty that were bigger. *Much* bigger.

I won't go so far as to say that the Henry's Fork is a better river than the Frying Pan—if for no other reason than that Bill Fitz-simmons, who owns the Taylor Creek fly shop on the banks of the Pan, would drive all the way down here to straighten me out—but I do make the obligatory pilgrimage to Idaho at least once a year. That's simply because fishermen must travel, it's part of the game, and when you go on the road you point your headlights in the direction of larger, rather than smaller, fish.

Being on the move is one of the charms of the sport, but you have to be careful to avoid the "never far enough north" syndrome. My father and I discovered this years ago in Minnesota. We lived in the southern part of the state, but drove north to fish in the summers. Way north, until we were far enough from home to feel the reality of a different place. We wanted to be up there where people went to fish.

Once we stopped in to see a friend of Dad's, only to find that he'd "gone north to fish." Dad turned to me and said, in his best allegorical tone, "Well, I guess you can never get far enough north." Then he gazed wistfully off through the trees in the general direction of the Arctic Circle, picturing his friend "out there" somewhere, standing on the pontoon of a floatplane catching fish. *Big* fish. Bigger than what we were catching, surely. I mean, he was farther north, right?

I remember that as one of those profound moments when you realize not only that your father is actually human, but that even the finest parts of life can hurt you; that it's possible to want too much of what you can't have. Dad died too young, but he was not a tragic character—quite the opposite, in fact. Still, he never did

catch *the* big fish, and there came a time when I thought I could
see that in his eyes. I'm not saying you shouldn't go. I think
you should go as far and as often as you can, just don't go staring
off into the trees like that when there are fish to be caught just
five minutes down the road.

The other way to catch the big ones is to actually fish for
them, which is something most of us don't do. We continue to
hope for big fish while fishing for the little ones. Some honestly
believe trophies are beyond their talents, but that is true only
of the very worst klutzes. Most know how to catch big fish, but
are just not up for it.

It's really pretty simple. First you gear up with a stout rod, a
heavy leader, and some huge flies. By huge I mean bigger than the
biggest ones you have now. Think of a big fish as a human being
with a salary in six figures. If you toss a penny on the sidewalk
to see what it will attract, you'll get kids and bums. A quarter will
get you teenagers and the occasional adult, although the latter
will glance around a time or two to make sure no one is looking
before he picks it up. A dollar will get you most people, but a
twenty-dollar bill will stop a Lincoln Continental in heavy traffic.

Next, find a good piece of water, ideally a lake or reservoir.
All things being equal, a good lake will hold bigger fish than a good
stream, with very large, productive rivers being the exception.
Pick one close to home, because you'll be spending a lot of time
there. If you must leave your own neighborhood, take the wall
tent, Winnebago, or whatever you have in the way of portable
luxury accommodations.

Dress warmly, because you'll be out all night and/or in the
worst possible weather. Dead of the night, dark of the moon, and
spitting rain is best.

Use a sink-tip or full sinking fly line to get deep and leave
the #16 dry flies at home. Not back in the car, I mean at home
where you can't get them if you weaken and decide to do a little
real fishing, just to break the monotony.

Don't fool around wading and casting from shore. Get into a
craft of some kind so you'll be mobile.

Finally, learn to sleep during the day and steel yourself for days, if not weeks, of dredging before you hook *the fish*.

Okay, maybe I'm being a little unfair, but that's how the real headhunters do it, day in and day out. It's not the only way to catch big fish, but it's how you make a career out of it. I can do it, but only for short stretches and only a few times in a season. Two straight days of kick-ass lunker hunting is about all I can handle, then I'm back to splitting the difference.

Splitting the difference means fishing all day like a gentleman on a good trout stream, taking a break for supper, and then coming back for two hours at night to cast a six-inch-long chipmunk fly to the stickiest logjam in the deepest bend pool in the whole river. Or maybe putting the bluegill rod away at dusk and coming back for a session with a 2/0, goggle-eyed bass bug and a jug of mosquito repellent. It must be done on occasion—especially when the conditions seem to beg for it.

Yet another way involves increasing your odds through precise timing. The prespawning congregation of fat, horney brown trout around the inlet to a lake may only last a week, but you can take your big fish then, and not just one, but several. A locally famous trophy hunter likes to go to the big reservoirs the night before the weekly stocking truck arrives. He says the big browns and rainbows eat the stockers like they were popcorn. They learn the stocking schedules and wait for the trucks.

Of course the hatches are the best; those few, famous, thick hatches and falls of large bugs that move the biggest fish to rise to the surface to dry flies. The most mythical of these is probably the hatch of the huge stoneflies on Montana rivers like the Madison and the Big Hole. The bug is the famous Pteronarcys something-or-other, known also as the giant salmon fly; the two-and-a-half-inch long, orange and black dry fly. Yes, I've seen the bug. In fact, I have one on the desk here in a bottle of formaldehyde. (I got it out to measure it in the interest of accuracy; I was going to say three inches.) Over the years I've hit the ends or the beginnings of this hatch on two rivers in Montana and one in Idaho, but have never seen it in its glory. I've heard the stories, though, from fishermen who are normally calm and droll, guys who shook me by the lapels and swore it was all true, as if they'd just seen Godzilla grazing in a field east of town. "Twenty-four-inch trout on every cast," they said, "cars skidding in squashed bugs on the highway . . ."

Relax. I believe it.

An even more interesting question than "What is a big fish?" or "How do you catch one?" is, "What will you do with it?"

Mounting it seems logical, and there is something smug about having the evidence right there on the wall. Not only that, it gives you a gracious introduction to the story. You don't have to go out of your way to bring it up, you just wait for someone to say, "Jeeze, nice fish," and there's your audience. Anyone who doesn't comment is probably a golfer and wouldn't understand anyway.

I have not been moved to have a fish mounted in recent years, but apparently that wasn't always true. My father swore that when I was just a tyke, no more than this high, I threw a fit because he refused to have a sunfish I'd caught in Wisconsin stuffed. "It wasn't even big enough to eat, and I threw it back," he said. "You raised hell for an hour."

What did I know? It was probably the fourth or fifth fish I'd ever caught and the first that wasn't a bullhead, but at the tender age of no more than five I knew what a mount was and I wanted one.

I still like mounts. I go out of my way to admire them (and not just to be polite, either) and have a special affection for old ratty ones that were caught by someone's daddy—who is now dead—forty years ago when everything, including the fishing, was better than it is now. But I don't have any myself.

There was a time when it was out of the question from an economic standpoint, and I'm not so sure that time has passed. I do now and then have a few extra bucks, but at five to eight dollars an inch, a 24-inch trout is worth two weeks on the road somewhere, during which time one might even catch yet *another* big fish.

I have a few photographs hanging around the place: the 8-pound rainbow from Kipps Lake, a 6-pounder from the nameless lake in Wyoming, etc. The 8-pound trout is my favorite because the photo was taken by Gary LaFontaine, a big-time famous fisherman whose name drops loudly and who also knows how to make a wide-angle lens add several pounds to an already heavy fish. "Aim his head up toward the camera a little more," he said.

I have so far released all of my truly big fish, unless you count bluegills and crappies, many of which I have fried in beer batter and eaten happily. A.K. killed a 5- or 6-pound brown two years ago, but only because it had taken the streamer deep in the gills and was clearly bleeding to death. It was delicious, by the way. Don't believe what they say about big fish not being good to eat.

I could get all moralistic about this business of not killing large fish, but the fact is, I've just never figured out how big a fish has to be before it absolutely demands to be stuffed. I have also learned that they don't look as big as they really are when they're mounted. You need a real pig to raise discerning eyebrows.

I've only met one fisherman who seemed to have that under control. He asked me, more or less in passing, if I knew where he could catch a 16-inch brook trout. It seemed like a reasonable, but still slightly odd, request, so I asked what he was up to. It seems he already had a rainbow, a brown, a yellowstone cutthroat, a golden, and a grayling—all exactly 16 inches long—mounted on the wall of his den. "Specimens," he said. "Archetypal examples of the trouts (and grayling) of North America, not trophies."

I liked that. It seemed rational, modest, scientific (but not *too* scientific); the well-bred answer to the problem of the trophy. I did actually have a suspicion about where a guy might catch a 16-inch brookie, but all I could bring myself to do was congratulate him on his finely honed aesthetics and wish him well. I'm a sucker for that kind of thing, but I'm not stupid.

So, how big should it be before you mount it? Hard to say. You could devise a rule of thumb, I suppose—if you didn't grunt when you lifted it in the net, it's not big enough—but that may miss the point. Unless you've got a wall full of stuffed fish, it should be a memento of a pinnacle in your angling career, and few of us are willing to admit that we've just caught the biggest fish we'll ever catch. With life as short as it is, that might be a milestone we don't care to pass.

Big fish are what we want, but they're like true love, success, lots of money, or maybe public office: we don't know *why* we want them, but we figure that will take care of itself if we ever connect. It will become obvious, won't it?

Maybe it's the quest that makes sense to us—the fragile balance between reality, possibility, and promise. The fisherman is privileged among human beings as one who can push his expectations with some hope of fulfillment. World peace and universal enlightenment are, I think, beyond us, but a fish that's an inch longer or an ounce heavier than the last one, well, shoot, that could happen.

Yet another problem with really big fish is that once spotted, they can't be hooked; once hooked, they can't be landed. As we all know, it takes tremendous fortitude to come away with anything like a straight face after being taken to the brink and then robbed of the satisfaction. Still, it's illustrative, possibly because it copies life in general so well.

Fly-fishing reveals character, and the bigger the fish the deeper the revelation. A potential wall hanger is not only a horrendous fish, it can also show your partners what you're made of.

Last summer A.K. and I were on our usual jaunt through Idaho and Montana when we hooked up with a gentleman named Bill Crabtree. Bill lives in Texas, but he spends several months in West Yellowstone, Montana, each year—at a place that's been in his family for several generations—to, as he puts it, "just sort of ease out a little, you know?"

One evening, after several days of fishing together, we decided to drive to a pond we knew of to see about getting into a big trout. Enormous fish live in this thing, but it's one of those places where you will probably not hook a fish, and if you do, you probably won't land it because it will be *too* big. For this reason, it's usually deserted, even though it's well known to fishermen in the area.

The main problem with landing the fish—over and above the usual problems one has with big, strong trout—is the weed beds.

They're wide and dense and ring the shore, and the gooey, unstable bottom makes wading unfeasible. If you work from shore and get into even a decent fish, he'll take you into the weeds, tangle himself up and break you off. All the big ones have done this a hundred times and are real good at it.

The solution is to fish from a belly boat. That way you stand a better chance of keeping the fish out of the weeds, and, failing that, you can at least go in after him with some hope of coming out again.

You fish a place like this on occasion, not so much to catch trout as to see how much adrenaline you can generate and how much disappointment you can stand. When you're alone you can swear and scream and thrash the water with your flippers when you lose a fish, but in company a modicum of restraint is expected.

It was just coming on evening—the best time—when we arrived at the pond, having hauled our float tubes, flippers, and rods down from the road. The smooth surface of the pond was unbroken by rise or boil, calmly reflecting the darkening sky and a range of mountains, but the knowledge of what swam there made the water seem to tingle with electricity. It was like the peacefulness of a hand grenade from which the pin has just been pulled. We rigged up slowly, with a studied casualness, although our eyes left the water only when necessary.

The first boil was unbelievably large. In most waters you'd assume it was a full-grown beaver, but not here. Here there were no beavers, probably because the trout have eaten them all. It caught us in various states of disarray: Bill and I were sitting on our tubes, half into and half out of our waders with rods still broken down. A.K. was still in hiking boots, but he had already strung up his rod and had a fly tied on—a #14 flying ant like the ones we'd seen on the water. A.K. always strings the rod first and he almost always starts with a dry fly.

He gave Bill and me a questioning glance. I shrugged and heard Bill say, "Hell, why not?"

A.K. worked out some line and cast ahead of the dissipating ripples that indicated the fish's direction. He barely had time to straighten the leader before one of the largest trout I've ever seen in the flesh swallowed the little dry fly with a great slurping and burbling of water.

A.K. set the hook, somewhat gingerly, and the fish shot to the deepest hole in the middle of the pond, tearing 6-weight line from the reel. And there he sat, immovable as a rock the size of a couch. The only sign of life was a petulant thrumming in the line. The fish wasn't scared, he was pissed.

"That was really stupid," A.K. said, half to himself. "Now what am I gonna do?"

Bill and I could think of nothing to say. Stupid, maybe, but there isn't a fisherman alive who wouldn't have cast to that trout from right there on shore. Anyone with the iron will it would have taken to suit up and get into the float tube first would be no fun to fish with.

He thought it over for a minute. It was painfully obvious.

"I'm gonna have to get into my waders and get into the belly boat and get the hell out there," he said. "Someone is gonna have to hold the rod for a minute."

Among fishermen there are moments of unspoken understanding; moments when there is no doubt whatsoever about what is going to happen next. It's enough to make you believe in fate.

A.K. looked over at Bill and me, who were both on our feet by then. Bill threw his hands in the air as if someone had just pointed a .44 magnum at his heart, did a smart about-face and walked off into the sagebrush and cactus. He knew what was about to transpire and he wanted no part of it.

That, of course, left the good old fishing partner.

A.K. gave me a silent look worthy of a Shakespearean actor. It said: this won't work, but it must be tried, and if the fish is lost it will be my own fault; I couldn't possibly blame you—but I will.

I wish I hadn't already put my flippers on, because the gravity of the situation called for something more dignified than for me to waddle over there like a duck and carefully take the rod.

A.K. was into his waders and flippers with one foot in the belly boat when I felt a ponderous wiggle in the line and the fly came loose.

It just came loose, honest.

A.K. froze in the unlikely posture of a man mounting a float tube. Bill was thirty yards out on the prairie, hands in his pockets, looking at the ground like a mourner at a funeral. The shadow of the mountains had swallowed the pond and a songbird twittered in that frantic way they have right at dusk—as if they haven't had enough to eat today and it's going to be a long, cold night.

And then Bill said, "I seen him break it off when you weren't looking."

The loss of a big fish, for whatever reason, reveals character. Much more so than the actual landing of a big fish, which only calls for a modicum of forgivably false humility.

Jay Allman and I were once fishing together on a lake known for its large rainbow trout; fish that were catchable, but that would come a few per day at best. And that's how they were coming to us. They were large enough—5 pounds and up—that the usual suspicion that there were even larger ones in there was muted. This thought is never absent from the mind of the fisherman, and it is always true, but there are times when it doesn't matter.

We were both in belly boats, and my back was to Jay, but it was one of those clear, calm, profoundly quiet western days, and I could clearly hear the zzzzup of his line as he set the hook and the growl of the reel as the fish bored off almost casually. On this particular lake, the hooking of a fish was an event, so I turned and gave Jay the clenched-fist salute still popular with aging counter-culture types. He returned it with a nod of the head, as his right hand was engaged in palming the reel.

I turned back to the line of cattails in front of me along which the grapefruit-sized head and shoulders of a large trout periodically broke the surface, now here, now there, eating God knew what in no discernible rhythm or pattern. The problem at hand was simply to make a cast that didn't line the fish and spook him. If the fly was the right one and I happened to inadvertently put it in front of him, he might even eat it, at which point it would become an entirely different game that I could also easily lose.

This calls for some concentration.

It was probably five minutes later when I glanced over at Jay. He was playing a fish.

"Another one," I yelled. "Quit showing off."

"Same one," he said, not looking up.

Indeed. For a fly-fisher of Jay's caliber to spend five minutes playing a single trout meant one thing: my presence with the camera would be required. I reeled in and paddled over, harboring visions of a *Sports Afield* cover shot. Blue sky, puffy clouds, red rock hills, big fish. Perfect.

I stopped at a respectful distance to watch. The rod was bent nearly double, the white fly line vanished into a depth of clear water that was hard to judge. And on the end of that line was another nine or ten feet of leader. The fish swam in wide, deep, lazy circles, slowly turning the belly boat with it. Jay was nowhere near panic, nor was he in much control, either.

This was a big, big, big, trout.

This was very serious business.

Now Jay adheres to the philosophy of land them or lose them, but don't mess around, so he was playing this fish to what he perceived as the limits of his tackle, trying to get it up off the bottom. It was working, but slowly.

Jay finally pumped the trout up to about six or eight feet, and we both caught a glimpse of him down there. We weren't really surprised at the nearly yard-long form because we'd both already taken some quite large fish there and none of them had been anywhere near this heavy or this tough.

It was about then that the rod went straight; Jay looked shocked for a few seconds, then bowed his head and sat there staring at the patch of orange material on the front of his tube where it says, "Inflate to 1½ psi during use; DO NOT OVERINFLATE" as if pondering the true meaning of the phrase.

After a minute or two of meditation, he looked up, smiled, and said, "Well, let's get another one."

That's all you can do. In fact, it's what you *must* do. It's one of the unwritten laws of the sport. There's obviously nothing to be gained by getting mad at yourself, and no one in his right mind would hold it against the fish.

IN
CAMP

nother wet, heavy snowfall that will turn
to mud in only a day or so. It's almost a
good rain, but not quite; a sure sign of
spring in Colorado. Every few years, around
this time, we'll get a snowstorm with
thunder and lightning. If I live to be a
hundred I'll never get used to that.

A friend of mine and several of his pals left two days ago on
their fifteenth annual Rite of Spring Camping Trip. It's a tradition
with them, and they now have volumes of stories about being
uncomfortably stranded in various parts of the Mountain West.

They clearly do this on purpose, although it seems to be an
unspoken agreement.

Day before yesterday they headed west over one of the passes
and into Utah, right into the storm that got here last night or
early this morning. Sure, I'm a little worried about him, but not
much. He's smart and has a strong survival mentality with the
training to back it up. I'd be more worried if he'd gone to New
York City for the weekend. And anyway, it's exactly what he
wanted: planned hardship in the Canyonlands.

I've never tried to horn in on this yearly campaign against the
weather, not because I'm not up for it (really) but because they
don't actually *do* anything. They just camp, although I'll grant you
that can be a full-time job at this time of year.

My own camping has taken a turn in the last decade or so. I don't just go camping like I once did, at least not very often. What I engage in now is what you might call "base camping," staying out in the woods in order to do something other than just be there. That something is usually fishing.

I do almost all of my base camping with A.K. these days, ever since that first trip to the Henry's Fork when it became evident that we had similar ideas about such things. A fairly high level of agreement in these matters is mandatory. You can go fishing with a guy who has a divergent style of fishing (within reason), but it's pretty hard to live with someone who disagrees with you about how the camp should be run.

Efficiency is our watchword. A fishing camp should function in such a way that the campers can fish rather than hang around doing chores and cooking gourmet meals. It should also go up quickly so you can fish the evening you get where you're going instead of pitching camp and then fishing in the morning.

Our motto is, First Things First.

Most of our camps in recent years have been next to the pickup, so that if the tent is the main lodge, then the camper shell, backed up to face the fire pit, serves as the storage shed. That kind of arrangement can be handy, but if you're not careful it can become *too* handy. With all that room it's tempting to bring all kinds of things you don't really need, even though all they'll do is get in the way. The things you might need, but probably—even hopefully—won't (like the first aid kit and the .357 magnum) are few enough not to be a problem.

We have the tent, sleeping bags, the modest but complete camp kitchen with utensils, Coleman stove, and bottle of whiskey, two coolers (one for beer, one for food), a cardboard box for canned provisions, several tarps, coil of rope, and the odd box containing knives, axes, screwdrivers, etc.

On some trips, especially the shorter ones, we bring a small stack of firewood from home so we don't have to waste time gathering it on the spot, and, of course, we seldom go anywhere for any length of time without the fly tying kits.

The rest of the stuff is fishing gear which, once camp is set up, is stowed at the back of the camper shell for easy access. A.K.'s stuff is on the left and mine is on the right.

All it takes is restraint and a clear vision of the problem at hand, which is to live on-site with as little fuss as possible and to catch fish, or, failing that, to at least give it one hell of a try. We've got it to where it takes no more than forty-five minutes to set up a camp, the only discussion being where the tent goes, and that can often be done with a point from one and a nod from the other. The camps vary some from place to place, but they're all pretty much the same. Coming back to them late in the evening is as familiar as entering your own darkened home at night. But then, what's home but a permanent camp?

This is something we just fell into and have never talked about much. We've never had to. Between us we probably have seventy years of camping experience, which, I like to think, allows us to differentiate between the necessary and the fluffy in terms of both chores and equipment.

Something else we just fell into is A.K. doing all the cooking. That's how it was the first time and how it's been ever since. Maybe it's because we use his kitchen; it's certainly not because he's a better cook.

Let me point out that I don't just lounge around with a mint julep while A.K. is slaving over a hot Coleman. In the morning I've got the sleeping bags aired out, the truck loaded, and lunches made by the time A.K. announces breakfast. In the evenings I've got the waders airing out, drinks made, and the fire going in time to sit and watch the stew come to a final simmer.

And A.K. is actually a pretty good camp cook. At this stage of the game it would be impertinent, if not insulting, for me to offer to take over for him.

If it sounds like there's very little camp lounging and fire-gazing, you're right, but there *is* a little of both. No outdoorsman worthy of the title is immune to the simple charms of camp.

These become apparent after supper with a few drinks around the campfire. Sometimes more than a few drinks. If we're out for a week, there's one night when we settle in and get seriously shit-faced. This usually happens at the end of a supremely good day, but not always. Good day or mediocre (I can't recall anything you could honestly call a "bad" day of fishing), it is a quietly joyous, celebratory drunk, the kind where at some point in the evening you look up at the clear Colorado, Idaho, or Montana sky to find that the satellites are standing still, but the stars are moving.

On normal camp evenings, the day's exploits are gone over in some detail, and philosophical implications surface. One night, after several straight days of sublime fishing on the Henry's Fork, we realized that we'd reached a new height in the area of losing count. Not only had we automatically lost track of the number of trout we'd caught, we suddenly couldn't remember how many times we'd been into the backing that day, something we'd normally keep track of.

At some point the plan for the following day is decided upon. This can be a long, involved sifting of options or it can be as simple as:

"Same place tomorrow?"

"You bet."

Some nights are spent examining questions. Why does the No-hackle mayfly dun pattern so often work better than a sparsely hackled standard fly? The hackle on the standard pattern represents legs, and, as A.K. has pointed out many times, "A mayfly *has* legs, right?"

It's a serious ponderment. I think it bothers him deeply.

Most topics naturally relate to fishing in one way or another, although we do sometimes take a few minutes to solve the world's problems. At night, around a campfire, a few minutes is all it takes.

A much more lengthy and heated discussion is likely to ensue over what the perfect fly rod for a certain stream or lake might be. We both still like to fish split cane rods, but have softened on that a little in recent years. In fact, I'm thinking of buying a 9½-foot, 6-weight graphite rod made by one of the famous manufacturers of such things. It's a fabulous rod, even though it's not made of bamboo. I'll have to get A.K.'s permission to do this, or if not permission, then at least some kind of grudging assent like, "Well, I guess if you want to fish with one of them plastic rods there's nothing I can do to stop you."

However the evening goes, someone is required to mention how great it is to be sitting around in camp, even if it's raining and we haven't caught any fish yet. After the appropriate pause in the conversation someone has to say, "Jeeze, this is great, ain't it?"

Another unspoken rule is that high-tone grammar is to be avoided wherever possible. The last thing you'd ever say in camp is, "That is something up with which I will not put."

There was a time, not all that many years ago, when I was into the classic off-trail backpacking head and thought that anyone who stayed in an official campground was a pussy. The *real* camper strained and sweated his way to the highest, most remote lakes where he caught cutthroat trout at the risk of life and limb. He ate cheap, starchy food, slept on the rocks under the sky, drank bourbon, and stayed up half the night howling at the moon. If he happened to meet a clean-cut hiker, he'd become sullen and dangerous-looking and slink off into the trees muttering about how the goddamned flatlanders ought to stay where they belonged.

Perfection was found only in solitude, with wild trout who had not seen the wader-clad legs of a human in at least a year. And that was not open for discussion.

But then, somewhere around my thirtieth birthday, it did become open for discussion, and I relented. It was as simple as that. Maybe I was getting a little older or something.

There were numbered parking spots with ready-made fire pits. Sometimes there was a faucet with cold water. Sometimes there were even bathrooms. Bathrooms! Well, at least the seats were cold.

"Of course, it's not real camping," I told myself, "but it *is* outside at least, and it's convenient, and it's a hell of a lot cheaper than a room."

And then I began to almost like it.

The campgrounds A.K. and I stay in now are filled mostly with fisherpeople, with the occasional vacationing family or retired couple thrown in for balance. Most lack what you'd call a real community spirit, but they're not unfriendly. There's even a sort of double-edged social hierarchy. The upper crust travels in monstrous Winnebagos or those big, shiny Air Stream trailers that sport, among other things, TV antennae. Sometimes these things travel in herds, and when a caravan of them descends on your campground it is referred to as an "aluminum hatch."

On the other end of the social ladder (not the "bottom," just the other end) are we tent campers. Pioneers. Tough guys. It may be my imagination, but I think we're accorded a certain respect. More than once we've had camper dwellers come over to visit, at which times we adopt the style of the clipped, one-word response.

"You guys fishing?"

"Yup."

"Doing any good?"

"Some."

And so on.

On occasion we hear what almost sounds like an apology.

"I'm not fishing myself this trip. It's"—he looks over his shoulder at Mom cooking dinner and the kids playing frisbee—"It's sort of a family vacation, you know?"

"Yup."

We've never talked about this, either, but I think it's a bit of compromise for A.K., too. Some nights when all the congratulations have been congratulated and the plans have all been made, we tell each other about our great, lonely camps of the past:

A.K. and Bob Fairchild on Hunt Creek back in Michigan. The little stretch of it between private deer camps that no one, and I mean no one, knew about back then. Opening day, cold, frost, or even a skiff of snow. No hatch. And, amazingly, a few brook and brown trout to flies. Not worms—flies. A modest creek with mostly okay fish, but wild, too. Sixteen- to eighteen-inch trout were sometimes caught. Big for Michigan. Hell, big for anywhere. And, naturally, not a soul within miles, not another track from that year on the obscure old logging road. The tall, ancient spruce trees around the fire pit. I've never seen it, but I can see it. I've heard about it a hundred times and could stand to hear about it again. I'm like a little kid with his favorite bedtime story.

"You forgot the part about the big trees, A.K."

"Oh yeah, the big trees, they were enormous . . ."

And some of my own, too:

The time Ed Engle and I stayed in the mountains until the food ran out and then stayed on eating nothing but trout—because the fishing was so good—and finally got so weak we just barely made it back to the car and then drove to the nearest truck stop and ate pancakes and eggs and then hamburgers and didn't even get sick.

Or the time on Goose Creek—also short of food—when we really wanted a trout to eat, but couldn't catch one. I made a fire to cook the last of the rice while Ed went back to the stream. He came back in twenty minutes with a great big trout, a rainbow as I recall. Said he'd been fishing with flies, but then noticed some grasshoppers. Since we were at an awfully high altitude for hoppers, he took it as a sign; caught one; apologized to it; hooked it right on his fly and caught the big trout on the first cast. He said he tried for another fish with another hopper, but didn't get one and knew why.

There was a long silence during which I thought, okay, I'll bite. "Why?" I asked.

"Because I forgot to apologize to the second grasshopper," he said as if it was obvious.

There's precious little hanging around the tent during daylight hours now, but on trips that stretch to a week or more, the obligatory camp afternoon is observed. This is when fly lines are cleaned and re-dressed, when the leaders are rebuilt, when certain lost items are looked for under the seats of the truck, and the general clutter that results from days of feverish fishing is straightened up.

A trip to the nearest town to do laundry and get supplies will be required.

Chances are flies will need to be tied; either replacements or new brainstorms. Tying in the wind—it's always windy when you try to tie outside—is feasible as long as you remember to weight down anything you're not holding onto. The flies produced are usable, but typically far short of gorgeous and can be readily identified later as "wind flies."

It's a lazy, pleasant couple of hours that still don't quite amount to goofing off. There are things to be done, even if the pace is slow. Just *sitting around* in camp is about as much fun as watching a bobber.

It occurs to me that it's been two seasons now since I've strapped the stuff on my back, hiked into some lake or stretch of stream in the mountains, and stayed there for a few days. About as long as you've had to make reservations for a wilderness campsite in the area near home where I used to go. I'll now pay good money to sleep in the dirt at a campground, but I find it difficult to make a reservation for an unspecified patch of rocks and pine needles in the wilderness area.

But there are still plenty of places around here where you can roll out your sleeping bag when and where the spirit moves you, and I think I'd better do that again soon. I don't want the sparse, remote camps to become campfire myths about my fading youth. I'm not that old yet.

I think I even know where to do it; it's where the four-wheel-drive track turns away from a certain little stream leaving a long stretch of water that few people fish. I'll bet I can talk A.K. into this with no trouble.

The campgrounds are convenient and comfortable, but I think it's a good idea to get back in the bushes now and then because, for me at least, "back in the bushes" is the real holy ground of this entire endeavor, the famous rivers notwithstanding.

And the fishing can be pretty good, too.

Koke decided to do that a couple of years ago and asked me to go with him. I wanted to, but couldn't for reasons that must have seemed important at the time, but that I can't remember now. What I remember now is wishing I'd gone along.

"Okay," he said, "but act as my check-in."

This is mandatory when you go into the woods alone, or even with a friend, for that matter. Tell someone where you're going and when you'll be back so they can mount the rescue if you *don't* come back.

The story that surfaced later was that Koke had gone into the canyon exactly where he said he was going to. It was a canyon with a little creek in it that held some nice trout, but that was seldom fished because of its ruggedness. He was going to be there for two or maybe three days, and it was on the first day that he tangled up in some rocks and took a very bad fall, the kind where your eyes go dark and your head buzzes. He later quoted himself as thinking, "Please, if anything is broken, let it be the fly rod."

That's pretty serious.

He was sore and bruised, but not mortally wounded, so he stayed and fished, as anyone in his right mind would have done. The weather, he said, was lousy about half of the time, and I remember sitting here in the comfort of the house, taking care of whatever was so important, wishing I was up there sitting in the rain with him.

I was gone when he came through here, but when I got home I found the following note tacked to my front door—the only clean limerick I've ever seen, which I have committed to memory:

Koke has returned from the gorge of St. Vrain
All weary and aching and racked with great pain
But his fond early wishes
Of many great fishes
Were born out through the sun, wind, and rain

Koke

Staying in the campgrounds is a little like fishing the Green Drake hatch on the Henry's Fork. You can't let the people get you down. In fact, you have to get into what it is: something of a mob scene with a mob scene's attendant charms.

One evening, in a campground populated by middle-aged fly-fishing types, including me and A.K., a handsome young couple in their early twenties arrived. They pulled in right next to us and so we waved, just to be polite. We were busy at the moment arguing over whether the wings on the flying ant fly pattern should be down or upright and whether they should be made of feathers or waffle-pattern plastic. Very deep stuff.

But the couple bounced over, introduced themselves, and said they were on their honeymoon. For some reason, people who are on their honeymoons want everyone they bump into to know about it.

A.K. nodded sagely, and I said, "Yup."

When they left, A.K. mentioned that the lady was a handsome specimen—something that wasn't lost on our other neighbors, either—and we went back to poking the fire and discussing ants. But you couldn't help but watch from the corner of your eye as they cooked up an intimate little dinner, opened a bottle of wine, and retired to their dome tent.

Now a dome tent, in case you've never noticed, has several tightly stretched panels that act like the speakers on your stereo set. They clearly broadcast whatever noises are being generated inside. There were whispers and giggles and the unmistakable sounds of sleeping bags being unzipped. A dozen fly-fishermen sitting around half a dozen campfires fell silent and listened.

Then A.K. turned to me and said, "I wish they'd get it over with so we could all get some sleep."

Some of our camping equipment goes back a long way, although only a few items go all the way back to the wood, canvas, and leather "conquer the wilderness" style of camping we were both brought up in. Now we're as much into nylon and aluminum as anyone. A.K. even has a new tent, a nice one, too, although it did have to be modified a bit.

The night it blew down in the windstorm and we had to sleep in the truck, he was sorely disappointed in it. The tent itself was okay, but the light aluminum poles were bent and twisted like the wreckage left by the Hindenburg.

Luckily that was to have been our last day belly boating the reservoir anyway. The next day we headed over to the Frying Pan River to do what A.K. refers to as "real" fly-fishing in running water. We stopped in Basalt, and A.K. asked around about an electrical supply place. There was one, which was lucky. It's a pretty small town. A.K. had the guy copy the tent poles in steel conduit. The guy was a fisherman and ended up doing it for what must have been no more than the cost of materials.

The new poles are heavy, but that doesn't matter because this is too big a tent to be backpacked anyway. It's a car tent, and with those steel poles the pickup will blow over before the tent comes down again.

I talk about "our" equipment, although most of what we use belongs to A.K. My stuff is mostly for backpacking, although some of it slops over nicely. I don't even own a tent, but then, why should I? A.K. has one.

ENOUGH FISH

The trout were enormous; long, fat, heavy. I couldn't see them at the moment in the dun-colored, predawn light, but they were there. I had seen them twice the day before, and, for once, it was the exactly logical place for them to be: in the deepest hole in the pond, in the thickest, most bug infested vegetation. Oh, they were there alright, at the long end of an easy cast in no more than four or five feet of water.

But maybe I should start a little closer to the beginning.

I'd heard about this place from a friend back in Colorado, a knowledgeable—though amateur—fisheries type who is one of the few fly-fishers I know who actually understands what the biologists tell him. And the ones he knows tell him plenty, knowing he'll use it to his own advantage, but wisely and reasonably.

My friend said he'd seen biologists' reports on the place showing huge brook trout at the top of an incredible food chain measured in tons of insects. Temperature, water chemistry, vegetation; everything was just right.

The ponds were in a mountain valley a good forty miles off the main highway in a little-traveled part of southern Montana. Much of the water in the valley, including two large lakes, was taken up by a waterfowl sanctuary where fishing was not permitted, but around the edge of the refuge were some spring-fed ponds and streams where you *could* fish.

My friend hadn't actually been to the place, so it was a story; one he knew I'd want to hear. I have a thing for ponds and another thing for brook trout. When the two came together in a single spot, he just had to call.

Thanks.

I ended up in the neighborhood of those ponds the following August on a long, circuitous trip that replaced the money in my wallet with a stack of nonresident fishing licenses and filled the less than airtight pickup camper with the fine, brown dust of four western states. The one scheduled stop was the Federation of Fly-Fishers Conclave in West Yellowstone, Montana, where I took part in a writer's panel and where my traveling partner, Jim Pruett, also had some business.

The conclave itself was just fine, but there was a slight pall over the proceedings in the form of poor fishing. The water was unusually low and none of the local rivers were much good. That, at least, was my experience and also the general consensus. A famous fisherman snuck out one afternoon to an equally famous river and showed up later at a party in the courtyard of a motel.

"How'd you do?" someone asked.

"Well," he said, as everyone stopped talking in anticipation of the master's pronouncement, "I caught an 18-inch rainbow . . . in 9-inch increments."

Disappointment isn't really the word. Fly-fishermen, a stoic bunch overall, seldom give in to that emotion in public. They either figure it out (keeping it to themselves when they do) or pile into their vehicles and move on. And they do both philosophically.

I asked around about the ponds, trying to do it quietly so as not to tip my hand. To my horror, everyone knew about them. In fact, the third person I asked handed me the current issue of the *West Yellowstone News*. He thought I'd be interested because the cover story dealt with the area I'd been asking about.

I ended up with the typical mesh of conflicting news and advice, mostly from people who knew the place but hadn't fished it in recent years. It was tough. It was easy. Everyone fished it.

No one fished it anymore. There were still big fish there. There were no big fish left; they'd all been caught, stuffed, and hung above mantels.

At the end of the conclave, as several hundred fly-fishers were preparing to leave the fly-fishing capital of the Free World for mostly undisclosed points in the further pursuit of trout, Jim and I split up. He was going to meet his brother on the Yellowstone River and I was heading home where, for various reasons, I was already overdue.

Head home indeed, with those ponds only an eighty-mile round trip off the straight shot back to Colorado? Right. The people back home who required my presence would have to buy "car trouble," and they *would* buy it, too. That's one of the advantages of driving a pickup that's older than the oldest dog you ever knew. "I'm surprised you made it back at all," someone would say.

It also just happened that I had a few days left on my Montana license; days of fishing I'd already paid for that would be sinful to waste.

I drove south into that knuckle-shaped end of Idaho and then, somewhere around Henry's Lake, turned northwest onto a dirt road that went, quietly and without fanfare, back into an unpaved corner of Montana. Jim Pruett is one of the best people I've ever traveled with, but, after some weeks, it was not unpleasant to be alone. Fishing is odd in that it's a solitary exercise that's usually practiced in groups. The camaraderie can be the best part, but it's also what sometimes leads to competition and even conceit.

Fishing alone can unmuddy the waters and allow you to return to the society of anglers with the capacity to remove the crap. For instance, A.K., who has been known to fish by himself happily for days on end, once invited someone to go fishing with us.

"Maybe you hadn't noticed," the man said, "but I don't fish with just anyone."

"You know, you're right," A.K. replied, "I *hadn't* noticed."

The road was a good one as dirt roads go, and I could have made good time except that I was apparently passing through open range. There were no signs to that effect, but I was slowed and stopped repeatedly by cattle standing in the way looking at me with that air of calm but uncomprehending proprietorship that has earned them the nickname "slow elk." It was a good sign, though. A sign of very thin traffic.

Part of the story I'd gotten from my friend on the ponds was that they were not heavily fished, and, although they were more widely known about than I was led to believe, I thought it could still be true. They were in a part of the state that the majority of tourists don't bother with and were near—but off the regular routes to—several famous rivers that take the brunt of the fishing pressure.

And they were ponds, after all, something most fly-fishers tend to pass up in favor of flowing water. Granted, rivers have their charms, but so do ponds. They can be isolated, hidden, even forgotten, in a way that can never happen with a stream, and there's the purely practical consideration that, all things being equal, a good pond can grow bigger fish than a good stream.

They can be a different kind of trout, too. Regardless of species, they're often deeper-bodied and rounder than river fish, and, psychologically, they can be more restless and curious. They're cruisers, hunters, not unlike bass.

The valley itself is a wide, flat, mountain-rimmed piece of land at an altitude that was not noted on my map. It felt high, though. The road had pointed gradually but steadily uphill for the last thirty-some miles. The one bit of information that had come up again and again involved some large brook trout that had been there once and might be there still.

I was looking for the Widow's Pool, which is known on maps and signs as Culver Pond. It was named, I was told, for the Widow Culver, although who Mrs. Culver was—or is—and why she has a trout pond named after her I don't know. That's the kind of background information a writer is supposed to jump on, but it seemed to me at the time that the pertinent journalistic facts involved these rumored big trout. And anyway, there was no local library or historical society to consult. In fact, there was little in the valley besides water, sagebrush, and the trumpeter swans for which the refuge had been established.

I found the pond after negotiating several unmarked dirt roads and parked the truck in a spot where others—but not too many others—had parked before. There were small but official-looking signs saying "Culver Pond" and "No Camping"—not a lot of information, but enough.

The pond looked a little questionable at first. It was shallow right where I'd stopped and had what looked like a clay bottom, though the water was spring-clear and there was healthy vegetation. No trout were immediately in evidence.

I was just about to take an inspection walk along the bank when another pickup arrived, this one sporting Montana plates. An older gentleman and an elderly bird dog got out. The former removed a strung-up spinning rod from the bed, glanced at my Colorado license plates, and stalked over to the water. He ignored my friendly wave, rather pointedly I thought.

The dog pissed on the right front tire of my truck and then followed his master at a respectable distance.

I approached slowly. In such situations, one adopts a studied casualness so as not to appear too eager, as if you're wandering around with nothing much in mind. You seldom fool anyone with this, but it has to be done.

By the time I'd ambled over to my colleague's side, he had baited up what looked and smelled like a pickled minnow and had lobbed it expertly out into the pond. I offered the dog my hand. He didn't seem overjoyed at meeting me; I ventured a pat, which he endured but didn't like much. Then, turning to the man, I said, "How ya doin'?"

"Uh," the man said, not looking away from his bobber.

He'd cast to a surprisingly deep hole where the bottom was dark with weeds. As I watched, a large shape materialized down there, and then another, and another. The hole was filled with a good dozen enormous trout—as big as the carp in an old farm bass pond, but *trout.*

I voiced a profanity under my breath, and, although the expression on my friend's face didn't change, his wrinkles grew visibly deeper.

The problem was obvious: I was standing there, complete with out-of-state license plates, in *his* spot, looking at *his* fish. If you're not a fisherman, the magnitude of this seemingly harmless fact will probably escape you.

It would have been useless to ask if he fished here often (though I had the feeling he did), or if the trout were brookies, or if he had ever caught any, or how big they really were. I did what common angling courtesy demanded. I thanked him and said I was going to go find a place to fish.

"Nice talking to you," I added.

I was in the cab of the truck with the motor running when the guy walked up. His face was still stern and his voice was gruff, but he said, "You see that cottonwood tree over there . . . ?" and launched into a clear and detailed set of directions to another good hole in the sprawling pond. "You try it over there," he said. "Maybe you'll get a nice one."

Then he turned and walked off without a nod, a tip of the hat, or anything.

So I followed his directions, which were accurate right down to the bush and fence post. Yes, he fished there often. At this point the dirt road was fifty yards from the water, but I could see the rises on the still surface of the pond. It was midmorning, maybe nine o'clock.

There was nothing man-made in sight except the road itself, not even a faint plume of dust out on the valley floor from another car. That was a good thing for two reasons: I would have the fish all to myself, and there was no one to see me as I doubled my usual rigging-up time by dropping every piece of gear I laid my hands on at least once, including the camera.

Excited? Well, maybe a little.

The bottom was clay, alright, sandy-gray, thick, sucking, claustrophobic clay. It was the kind of goo you stop sinking in tentatively and that leaves you with the feeling you could start again at any second, finally to go out of sight altogether, leaving nothing but a floating hat and an abandoned truck. That's why I didn't wade out as far as I'd have liked to. There were plenty of weeds on the bottom but, for some reason, their root systems gave no support. This is the kind of situation where if you lose your balance you *will* fall in the water, simply because it will take too long to extricate your foot from the muck to take that saving, balancing step backwards.

I was out far enough to see that the trout were rising and boiling along the edge of a dropoff where the shelf of shallow, weedy bottom I was mired in gave way to darker water. There were scattered Callibaetis mayfly duns on the water, about a size 14 or 16.

If I had to have a favorite mayfly, it would be this speckled dun. Mayflies in general seem Victorian, with more parts and more exaggerated proportions than they really need. Add to that the Baroque speckling pattern on the Callibaetis wing, and you have a creature whose beauty goes way beyond mere function. In that way, they're like the trout themselves.

They're a still-water bug, common on many trout lakes, and they hatch in a sporadic, surging way so there's never a uniform number of them on the water. First there's a lot, then there's a few, then there's a whole bunch of them again. It's as if they're trying to confuse the trout so a few of them will get away, and I've heard it said this is exactly what they're up to. It's a survival tactic.

The trout were cruising just below the surface, some of the larger ones leaving wakes. About one in three rose to the surface to take the winged flies—their "glups" were clearly audible in the still air—while the rest boiled under the surface taking emergers. I tied on a #14 Hares Ear Soft Hackle, a kind of universal emerger pattern, thinking, "It can't be this easy, but you have to start somewhere."

It was that easy. On the second crawling retrieve the leader stopped with a good deal of authority, and I set up on what felt like roughly two pounds of fish. The trout stayed in the water, boring instead of jumping. I played him hard and lost him in the thick weeds six feet in front of me.

"Well, of course, you idiot," I thought. "What did you expect?"

With a fresh fly of the same pattern on, I picked out what looked like a sizable fish, cast a few feet ahead of him, and felt the weight on the second slow strip. I played him out in the open water, and when his head came up I skidded him over to the net just like I knew what I was doing.

A brook trout, 14 or 15 inches long, deep-bellied, deeply colored from the rich water and a good diet. Not the mythic wall hanger, but a trout, and a good one.

There followed an hour and a half of steady fishing to cruisers, during which I lost some and landed plenty. Most were respectable keepers at 12 to 14 inches, though I didn't keep any, and a few ran up to 16, 17, and, I believe, 18 inches. I don't usually stop to measure fish in the heat of things, but I was fishing an old Granger 8½-foot, 4-weight cane rod with 56 intermediate wraps from cork to tip, 18 on the butt section. I used the first few of these as a rough scale, but back on the tailgate of the truck with a tape measure, I couldn't remember if the biggest trout had gone nearly to the fourth wrap or just past the third. In the finest angling tradition, I chose the larger number.

Yes sir, an 18-inch brook trout.

It ended as Callibaetis hatches do; petering off, surging back, weaker each time, ending with the odd small fish rising well out of casting range.

It was barely noon, although it seemed like a whole day had gone by, so I made a sandwich, had a warm beer, and then drove around the valley watching the swans and looking at other ponds where no trout rose. My map showed a fair-sized lake at the end of a long, twisting road up the northern slope of hills, so I drove up there and found, lo and behold, a little lodge. There were five or six small cabins and a main building inside of which was a bar and many mounted fish.

By reflex, I sat down and ordered a beer, a cold one this time, from Greg Williams, bartender, manager, head guide, etc., and commenced to learn that in the surrounding lakes, ponds, and streams one could catch rainbows, cutthroats, brook trout, grayling, and lake trout. No, they weren't *all* huge, but the ones hanging on the wall were, and so were the ones held by grinning clients in the regulation collection of snapshots.

Nor was the area fished very heavily, being, as Greg suggested, not quite in synch with the mass mental picture of Idaho/Montana trout fishing with its MacKenzie boats and wide rivers. But those who did fish it were known to come back. The cabins were regularly occupied.

In the fall there was good hunting for elk, deer, and grouse, with bears in evidence.

I went to the bathroom, but couldn't find the light switch. Greg came in behind me and lit an oil lamp. No electricity except for a generator to cool the beer.

The closest phone?

"About fifty miles."

"Sure I'll have another beer," I said, and the plot began to hatch. I'd drive home and pick up a few things—rifle, shotgun, more fishing gear, winter clothes. I'd empty the savings account, rescue the dog from the kennel, and drive back. I could slide in and out of town in early morning so as not to be noticed and as far as anyone would know, I would just not have come back at all. Jim would say he'd seen me last in West Yellowstone.

No one would find me. Not the I.R.S., not my editor at the newspaper, not even A.K. would know where to look. I could send him a farewell postcard, though, with the confidence that he'd smile, burn it in the fireplace and never say a word.

Somewhere in there I switched from beer to coffee so I'd be able to drive, even though there was damned little to run into. Then, without entirely dismissing the plan, but considering the possibility that I'd been on the road a little too long, I drove back to the hole on Culver Pond that held the big trout, all of which had been clearly longer than 18 inches. Much longer.

The old man and the dog were gone, which meant, I suspected, that the fishing was better there in the morning than in the evening. The trout were still there, looming in and out of the weed-shapes; much put-upon trout that would show themselves, but that were not about to do anything stupid.

On a stouter rod and a sink-tip line, I tried the Hares Ear Soft Hackle, then a more accurate mayfly nymph, then a damselfly nymph, then a crawdad pattern, then three different streamers in panicky succession. With each fly change my stomach clutched a little tighter with a combination of hunger and failure.

After dark, resigned, I drove to the closest turnout that didn't say "No Camping," warmed a can of beans, ate, and slept.

I was back before dawn with a thermos of fresh camp coffee and some two-day-old West Yellowstone doughnuts. I couldn't see the trout for lack of light, but they were there, no doubt about it. They were the kind of fish that are always there; so big and so close to uncatchable they're almost not real.

Standing out there in the cold half-darkness it occurred to me that if I left then I could be home in twelve hours, scratching the dog behind the ears, listening to several weeks of tape on the answering machine, and going through a stack of mail looking for checks. I found myself wondering, in a strangely detached way, if I'd be staying or leaving.

Maybe what you ask yourself at a time like this is, "Why am I doing this?"

Challenge? Excitement? Relaxation? Ambition? (or lack of ambition?) To "get away?" To get away from *what?*

Is it all just an excuse to drive hundreds of miles on strange roads, drink, eat poorly, not bathe, and come off generally as some kind of harmless, aging beatnik? And if it is, so what? You couldn't do any of this without the fish, but how large a part do the fish actually play?

More than one outdoor magazine editor will tell you, "We're not too interested in 'why I fish' stories." As I once heard it put, "Our readers already know why *they* fish and they don't much care why *you* do." Based on some years of talking to fishermen, I'd have to admit that's about the size of it.

There's a good deal of latitude in outdoor writing. It's the original Gonzo journalism, after all, Dr. Hunter S. Thompson notwithstanding. Another editor once said his magazine seldom accepts fiction, "except what normally occurs in any fishing story." But one thing that doesn't seem to be permissible in angling literature is to just walk away from good fishing for no other reason than that you've had enough.

Is it possible to have caught enough fish, at least for the moment? You know you can't catch them all, and there's no reason why you should want to. A year ago—maybe even to the day—I was standing at another piece of water puzzling over other fish. No, I don't remember the exact situation, but it was August; what

else would I have been doing? Given half a break, I'll be doing the
same thing somewhere else a year from now, both diminished
and enriched by another season. Definitely older, possibly wiser—
if I've paid attention.

It was just dawn when I drove off in the general direction of
home without so much as having strung up a rod. I was looking
forward to the long haul across the expanse of eastern Wyoming, a
stretch of country that some have called featureless, but which is,
in fact, filled with tranquillity. My only regret was that I wouldn't
be able to see the old man's face when he pulled in later that
morning to find that the guy from Colorado wasn't fishing his spot.